Entangle

Entangled Empathy

An Alternative Ethic for Our Relationships with Animals

LORI GRUEN

Lantern Books ● New York
A Division of Booklight Inc.

2015
Lantern Books
128 Second Place
Brooklyn, NY 11231
www.lanternbooks.com

Printed in the United States of America

The cover photo by Jo-Anne McArthur/We Animals depicts Rachel Hogan of Ape Action Africa in Cameroon with rescued gorillas.

Library of Congress Cataloging-in-Publication Data

Gruen, Lori.
Entangled empathy : an alternative ethic for our relationships with animals / Lori Gruen.
        pages cm
 Includes bibliographical references.
 ISBN 978-1-59056-487-5 (pbk. : alk. paper)—ISBN 978-1-59056-488-2 (ebook)
 1. Animal welfare—Moral and ethical aspects. 2. Animal rights. 3. Human–animal relationships. I. Title.
 HV4708.G779 2015
 179'.3—dc23

                    2014049780

Contents

Preface

❧ ❧ ❧

Marc Bekoff

𝒮O MANY DISCUSSIONS about our relationships with other animals focus on "rights" or "welfare." I prefer to think in broader terms, about compassionate living. As we destroy the homes of billions of nonhuman animals, forcing them into closer, often fatal, contact with humans who themselves don't have their rights acknowledged, we need to address more adequately the growing conflicts that are leading to the demise of our planet and all of her inhabitants.

Lori Gruen's *Entangled Empathy* provides a powerful new way of thinking about our ethical responsibility to protect animals. With sensitivity and passion, Gruen helps us go deeper into understanding the ways that empathy can guide us to resolve conflicts among humans and between humans and other animals, and act to try to stem the destructive tides.

As a scientist who has spent thousands of hours observing animals, I have long valued empathy as a tool in my own work. But scientists are taught not to empathize, but rather to remain detached and "objective" in observations of other animals. Naming animals and assigning them personalities were widely frowned upon as being "too anthropomorphic" and non-scientific. But, this is where science has gone wrong.

I would not have been able to understand and appreciate many different patterns of behavior if I weren't empathizing with the animals I studied. Empathy lays the groundwork for figuring out what questions to ask and how to go about answering them.

Empathy is not simply a necessary perspective for scientific understanding. It also has deep evolutionary roots. Jean Decety, a neuroscientist, recently concluded that, "There is strong evidence that empathy has deep evolutionary, biochemical, and neurological underpinnings. Even the most advanced forms of empathy in humans are built on more basic forms and remain connected to core mechanisms associated with affective communication, social attachment, and parental care."[1]

Empathy is something that is shared with other animals who don't practice science as we know it. Many studies have shown that nonhuman primates, dogs, mice, rats, elephants, and chickens all engage in empathetic behavior. This really shouldn't be too surprising given the role empathy plays in social cooperation. I couldn't explain social play in which individuals cooperate to play fairly with one another without attributing empathy to other animals.

In my long-term research projects studying the details of social play in domestic dogs and wild canids, I learned that although play is fun, it is also serious business. When canids—members of the dog family—and other animals play, they use actions such as vigorous biting, mounting, and body slamming that could be easily misinterpreted. So it is important for them to communicate clearly what they want and expect. Animals at play are constantly working to understand and follow the rules and to communicate their intentions to play fairly. They fine-tune their behavior on the run, carefully monitoring the behavior of their play partners and paying close attention to infractions of the agreed-upon rules. Four basic aspects of fair play in animals are: ask first, be honest, follow the rules, and admit you're wrong. When the rules are violated, and when fairness breaks down, so does play. For example, wild coyote youngsters who don't play fair often find themselves excluded from their group and suffer higher mortality rates than those who remain with family and friends.

Empathy allows individuals to form and maintain social bonds and to understand and negotiate their social relationships. Nonhuman animal beings, like human beings, form intricate networks of relationships and live by rules that maintain a stable society. Without empathy, we would not be able to navigate our social worlds. So many human problems could be avoided and addressed if we were able to deepen our empathetic engagement with one another and the rest of nature.

Entangled Empathy guides us in doing just that and I hope it enjoys the wide readership that it deserves. A focus on empathy is just what is needed to make the world a better place for all animals, human and nonhuman alike. ❖

Marc Bekoff is author of Rewilding Our Hearts: Building Pathways of Compassion and Coexistence *(Novato, California: New World Library, 2014). He lives in Boulder, Colorado.*

1. "The Neuroevolution of Empathy," *Annals of the New York Academy of Science* 2011 Aug; 1231: 35–45.

Foreword

～～～

Amy Fultz and Cathy Willis Spraetz

$\mathscr{F}$EW OF US take the time to reflect on empathy—what it is, when it is important, what it can teach us. In this book, Lori Gruen explores the various ways that empathy works in our entangled relationships with each other as well as with other animals we have welcomed into our lives.

Working at Chimp Haven, a sanctuary for chimpanzees retired from biomedical research, the entertainment industry, and the pet trade, we have many opportunities to experience empathy, not only chimpanzee to chimpanzee, but also between chimpanzees and humans.

Chimp Haven's reason for existence is to serve the chimpanzees in our care and attend to their physical and psychological needs. In order to attend to those needs we are obliged to understand the lives of chimpanzees in both the wild and captivity. There are moments when, in order to figure out what a chimpanzee is trying to communicate, or why a chimpanzee is behaving in a particular manner, we have to consider the chimpanzees' perspective and "put ourselves in their place."

Kidd was retired to Chimp Haven from biomedical research. Around six months after his arrival, he began showing signs of stress and abnormal behavior, screaming and biting his own toes and hands. After witnessing this many times, we realized that Kidd was displaying these behaviors when the hose used to clean the chimpanzee areas was near him. At Chimp Haven, the chimpanzees are moved to different rooms or, when temperatures allow, outdoors when we clean the indoor areas, but the hoses sometimes need to be nearby. We wondered why this would cause Kidd stress.

Putting ourselves in Kidd's place and remembering his background gave us the answer. At one time, it was common practice for research facilities, such as the one Kidd came from, to clean the rooms while the chimpanzees were still in them! This involved spraying water from a high-pressure hose into a small indoor enclosure to remove waste material. Chimpanzees are typically afraid of water, or at least they avoid it. Some became aggressive when their enclosures were being washed and this was most likely because they were frightened and couldn't get away. They feared they might get sprayed by the hose directly. These must have been Kidd's fears as well. By giving him additional rooms to move into farther from the hose and being cognizant of this fear, we helped reduce his stress so that he no longer injures himself.

We regularly see sick chimpanzees being helped by a friend or a group-mate to access favored foods or treats. We've also seen chimpanzees show awareness of another individual's limitations, as in the case of Betsy who is elderly and arthritic. Her friend Sheena waits patiently for her as she makes her way, slowly and deliberately, out of the habitat to inside housing.

A striking example of what we think of as empathy

between chimpanzees occurs when orphaned chimpanzees are cared for by others. When four-year-old Tracy lost her mother, Teresa, to a degenerative spine disease, Tracy's groupmate Suzanna quickly took over as her surrogate—carrying, protecting, and grooming her. In addition, Tracy's groupmates also became friendlier toward Tracy, giving her more positive attention and attending to her needs.

In the wild, chimpanzees live in large groups of both males and females and old and young. With a large enough group in captivity, chimpanzees can engage in "fission–fusion" dynamics, as they would in the wild—opting to spend most of their time within a small group of friends, but interacting with the larger group at different times. This allows the captive chimpanzees to experience rich social relations. At Chimp Haven we are regularly involved in formal "introductions," as we seek to make space for newly retired chimpanzees and attempt to enrich the lives of the chimps by expanding their groups.

Chimpanzees are often aggressive during their first meetings with other chimpanzees. This aggression is typical, as they are territorial in the wild and do not often welcome strangers. Recently, we introduced new chimpanzees to two special-needs males, Chaka and Ned. At some time in their past history, both had sustained head injuries that made it difficult for them to navigate their environment. We were amazed by the way the other chimpanzees gently and calmly approached both Chaka and Ned, seemingly understanding that Chaka and Ned experienced the world differently.

There are also interactions in which chimpanzees

show empathy toward people—especially those they are most familiar with. Male chimpanzees perform aggressive territorial "displays," showing everyone how big, powerful, and strong they are. And no one does that more vigorously than Hamlet, a young male who displays frequently at staff members and visitors alike. One of our employees, who has known Hamlet for decades, recently had to have an emergency appendectomy. The day she returned to work and went to visit Hamlet, he did not display at her, but instead sat down calmly and pointed at her abdomen. Clearly, Hamlet knew something had happened and was showing something like empathetic concern for her.

We often see chimpanzees display happiness and joy at seeing old friends. When Dr. Gruen made one of her many trips to Chimp Haven, Emma, a young female, illustrated this beautifully by gathering a bouquet of "flowers" from her enclosure and handing it to Lori as if to say "welcome back!"

In the past, having empathy for another species was frowned upon, especially for scientists. In an effort to make science objective, scientists were often encouraged to look only at animal behaviors—what could be observed and described objectively—and not the contexts in which these behaviors may have occurred or the possible reasons why they were occurring. Dr. Jane Goodall was herself criticized for giving the chimpanzees names, and to this day there are others who feel that the animals in their care should not be named as they believe it undermines their objectivity and that of their staff members. In a world where many studies have proved repeatedly the individuality of animals of many different species, it is surprising that this viewpoint still exists. Dr. Goodall believes that it is crucial to empathize with other species; it gives us a starting point for understanding. She often tried to take the point of view of the chimpanzees she was observing, and once said, "I think those two are behaving like that because that's how I would behave in that situation," which gave her something to test in a more empirical manner.

To provide the very best care for a species as psychologically and socially complex as chimpanzees, we need to continuously assess our own motives and reactions and hone our empathetic skill. This skill can be improved upon when we pay attention to the details we glean from our initial reactions and combine that understanding with what we know scientifically and observationally about the chimpanzees. This involves being aware of the environment and context of any given situation as well as the particular personalities and experiences of those for whom we care. And it calls us to be aware of ourselves and how we are both similar to and different from those we are empathizing with.

For those of us who wish to know and understand more about the lives and wellbeing of other animals, *Entangled Empathy* offers us an opportunity to look for and practice empathy in all that we do. ❖

*Amy Fultz is Director of Behavior, Research and Education, and **Cathy Willis Spraetz** is President and Chief Executive Officer at Chimp Haven, Shreveport, Louisiana.*

Introduction

꙳꙳꙳

 FIRST BEGAN thinking about my relationships with other animals from an ethical perspective after reading Peter Singer's *Animal Liberation* while I was in a philosophy class in college. I completely agreed with him that unnecessary suffering is bad and that if we can work to end that suffering without thereby foregoing anything of greater value, we really should do so. Like many people, I had no idea how much suffering and violence were required to convert animal bodies into food, and when I learned I became vegetarian and, soon after, vegan. I also decided to become a philosopher.

But before getting my Ph.D. in philosophy, I took a break from school to work full time in the animal liberation movement. It was then that two things began to dawn on me. First, the idea of "animal suffering" was much too general and broad. The general slogans of the animal movement didn't convey any of the depth of the experiences particular chickens, chimpanzees, cows, cats, and others had—experiences that made their suffering specific for them, from their point of view. And this was related to the second thing that dawned on me: It was hard to get other people to see what was wrong with causing animals to suffer just by telling them that animals suffer. I started to have the idea that if we really wanted to make a positive difference for other animals we needed to acknowledge that we are *already* in relationships with other animals, and for the most part, they aren't good relationships. We needed to radically rethink these relationships if we wanted to improve everyone's wellbeing.

I was flattered that Peter asked me to write the chapter "Animals" in his *Companion to Ethics*, published in 1991. I hadn't yet returned to graduate school but I was imagining how we might think differently to try to overcome the limitations with the popular framing of animal liberation. Inspired by the work of Marti Kheel, I wrote a section on sympathy in that chapter. Since that early article, I have been refining what I now call *entangled empathy* and exploring the ways it can help us rethink our relationships.

This book draws on the work I have done over the last twenty-five years. Sometimes I repeat what I wrote in papers I published about empathy; other times I revise, amend, or deepen what I have said; and some of what I say here I am saying for the first time. I have a feeling this will not be my last word on the subject either, but it does represent a coherent and, I hope, helpful view. I have tried throughout the book to keep philosophical jargon to a minimum and to make my thoughts accessible to anyone who is interested in joining me in the process of thinking differently.

In the first chapter I analyze the problems with traditional ethical theories upon which much of the animal liberation movement relies and discuss ethics of care, a broad theoretical framework in which entangled empathy fits. In Chapter 2 I discuss what empathy is and explore various, related ideas as well as misconceptions about how empathy works. In the third chapter I present entangled empathy, explore its possibilities and its limits. In Chapter 4 I discuss the ways that entangled empathy can go wrong and how we can improve our entangled empathetic engagement with each other and other animals.

We seem to know what empathy is but our ideas vary a lot. I'll be discussing the various ways that the concept and experiences of empathy have been understood in the pages that follow. I'll use the adjective "empathetic" rather than "empathic," although both are equally meaningful. Entangled empathy may or may not match your own view of empathy, so in the hopes of making my view clear, here is a definition that it might be useful to turn back to occasionally:

Entangled Empathy (enˈtaNGgəldˈempəTHē): a type of caring perception focused on attending to another's experience of wellbeing. An experiential process involving a blend of emotion and cognition in which we recognize we are in relationships with others and are called upon to be responsive and responsible in these relationships by attending to another's needs, interests, desires, vulnerabilities, hopes, and sensitivities. ❖

Chapter 1

❧❧❧

SEEKING AN ALTERNATIVE ETHIC

I FEEL OVERWHELMED by the problems that humans and other animals face in the world today. An estimated 20,000 children die every day from hunger. Over a billion people lack access to minimal health care. Nearly 750 million people lack access to clean water sources, and this, combined with poor sanitation, kills over 12 million people annually. Over 35 million people across the globe are living with HIV/AIDS and nearly two million die from it every year. In Africa, a child dies every minute from malaria, a readily preventable and curable disease. Almost half of the world's population—over three billion people—live on less than $2.50 a day, and at least 80 percent of humanity lives on less than US $10 a day. The top one percent of the world's richest people owns 65 times the total wealth of the bottom half of the global population, which owns the same amount cumulatively as the 85 wealthiest individuals. There are over 45 million forcibly displaced persons worldwide. Millions of people are incarcerated or denied their freedom and dignity because they are different from those in power. Scientists estimate that between 150 and 200 species of life become extinct daily; this unprecedented episode of extinction is more rapid than anything the globe has experienced since the vanishing of the dinosaurs. Every single day I feel as if I have to work to avoid being bombarded by reports of atrocities, from sexual abuse to wrongful imprisonment, from genocide to infanticide.[1]

Although hatred, violence, greed, and indifference cause so much suffering for humans across the globe, in sheer numbers the situation for other animals is far worse. Over 100 billion animals, including sea animals, are killed for food around the world annually. The devastating environmental and climatic impacts of this mass production and destruction of animals, though ignored by too many environmentalists, has led some to call for cutting back on or eliminating animal consumption altogether. An estimated 115 million animals—including mice, rats, birds, fish, rabbits, guinea pigs, dogs, cats, and nonhuman primates—are used in laboratory experiments each year.[2] Some of the most historically grotesque research that involved separating infant monkeys from their mothers to explore the psychological devastation that results has started up again at the University of Wisconsin.[3] Elephants, gorillas, chimpanzees, rhinoceroses, and other large mammals are being poached into extinction.[4] If drastic measures aren't taken, orangutans may die out in the next decade as their habitat is destroyed to make way for more palm oil plantations.[5] Dozens of species of birds and reptiles are facing extinction. Human activities—including emitting greenhouse gases, forest and mineral extraction, and increased development—are destroying habitats for millions of nonhuman beings.

I understand the impulse to turn away from thinking

about just how horrible things are; it can feel hopeless. But rather than turning away, I turned toward the study of ethics with the hope that it would help me not only think more clearly about these problems, but also empower me to begin to formulate solutions. I recognize that this choice may seem odd and that many people think ethical reflections by philosophers are too academic and not usually of much use in "the real world."[6] I've heard people say that arguing about what is good or right or just is an idle pastime for a very small group of relatively privileged theorists. Others have told me that they see the state of the world as inevitable, that nothing can be done to make changes for the better, and so there is no reason for thinking about these matters from an ethical point of view at all. Some people have even said that because the problems of the world are unavoidable it would be best for the small group of us who worry about them to keep quiet and not mention how terrible things are. Recognizing the futility of efforts to improve things, they argue, just makes people feel useless and enhances despair. Nonetheless, I continue to believe that together we can change the world and that ethical thinking can help.

Ethics is concerned with determining which actions are right and which are wrong, what actions are permissible and what are impermissible. Those of us who work in ethics try to articulate, develop, and refine action-guiding theories that can help us address, and ideally resolve, moral problems.[7] Ethical theory should help guide our actions toward making the world better. In the face of the bewildering practical complexities associated with solving the world's problems, ethical theory should both motivate us and point us in the direction of what to do.

Unfortunately, it rarely does either.

The Failure of Traditional Ethical Theory

The failure of ethical theory has been the subject of much debate within philosophy, within animal studies, and among activists looking for guidance. Sometimes ethical theory is viewed with ironic skepticism. Critics have suggested that ethical theory has become the domain of sanctimonious moralizers, who rarely if ever practice what they preach or, if they do, are almost impossible to associate with! In the hands of academic philosophers, ethical theory has become a rarefied business, with little relevance to the actual people confronting moral issues. Academic philosophers too often place themselves outside the moral fray of struggle and compromise, and prescribe action without any real understanding of the complexity of the moral problems their theories are designed to illuminate and potentially resolve.

One common strategy that philosophers who work in ethics use is to set complexity aside, since it muddies the force of ethical arguments—arguments that are based on abstract, universal principles deduced through careful, albeit detached, reasoning. Here are a couple of notable examples. The first comes from a now-famous article by Peter Singer from 1972 entitled "Famine, Affluence, and Morality":

1. Suffering and death from absolute poverty and lack of food, shelter, and medical care are bad.

2. If it is in our power to prevent something bad from happening, without sacrificing anything of comparable moral importance, we ought to do it.

3. Given our level of affluence, we can do much more without making too great a sacrifice.

4. We ought to be doing more than we are currently.[8]

Once we determine what counts as a sacrifice, how to compare the moral significance of various actions, and get specific about what "doing much more" amounts to, it is hard to find flaw in this reasoning. It is also hard to criticize the argument for failing to guide action. It clearly can when the details are worked out.

Here is another, more recent example from Jeff McMahan:

1. The mass production and destruction of animals in order to eat them causes tremendous, unjustified suffering.

2. So-called "humane farming" may minimize some of the pain of industrial animal production, but animals still suffer in the process of being slaughtered. They are also denied the future pleasant experiences they would have had if they weren't prematurely killed to be eaten.

3. Both of these forms of animal production are

not ethically justifiable because we are causing unnecessary pain and depriving animals of future pleasurable experiences.

4. Suppose that we could create a breed of animals genetically programmed to die at a comparatively early age, when their meat would taste best.

5. Suppose further that we cause these animals to exist and raise them in conditions in which they are happy and respected before they die painless deaths.

6. If 4 and 5 occur, we are not causing unnecessary pain and we are not depriving animals of future pleasurable experiences they would otherwise have.

7. Thus, there is nothing wrong with collecting the bodies and eating these animals "the nice way."

I have tremendous respect for both Peter Singer and Jeff McMahan, both of whom have had a significant impact in helping people think differently about their responsibilities in the face of moral crises that result from inequality and violence. But I am increasingly dissatisfied with this style of argumentation. For all their clarity, these arguments, which are perfect examples of the kinds of arguments that are most often made in ethics, force us to focus in too narrow a way and they flatten or erase the complexity of actual moral problems. Singer's argument doesn't adequately recognize the particular concerns, interests, worries, attitudes, sympathies, or sensitivities of actual people deciding what to do when confronting the suffering and death caused by poverty, for example. Nor does it adequately take into account the experiences of those suffering and dying. This type of argumentation ignores the genesis, quality, context, and significance of particular concerns, interests, worries, sympathies, etc., and it cannot help but do so, hence the gap between theory and experience. McMahan's argument focuses on a hypothetical case that is very far-fetched and it fails to explore the ways in which keeping animals in the category of "edible" fundamentally distorts our relationships with them.[9]

This sort of abstract reasoning also highlights the detached and mechanical nature of traditional ethical argumentation. A sophisticated computer program or robot could identify where suffering from absolute poverty is occurring, calculate whether one individual doing something about it would, all things considered, be better or worse, and print out a prescription for action. This sort of reasoning not only reduces moral agents to calculators but it stereotypes the individuals suffering as objects to be aided. They are nameless and interchangeable—we only recognize them as victims of absolute poverty, or in the case of animals, as food that is either treated nicely or cruelly. We don't attend to the particularities of their lives in their communities and the relationships they are in, and we can easily avoid such questions when we formulate our ethical deliberation in abstract ways. But it is often the richness of the individual's experiences and relationships that helps us to understand what makes life meaningful, interesting, and valuable to them, and thus what is lost or gained when we act or fail to act. Paying attention to the particularities can also help us keep in check condescending attitudes, culturally imperialistic judgments, and more pernicious forms of anthropocentrism.

Ethical reasoning of this sort involves what ecofeminist Marti Kheel called "truncated narratives." The standard form of ethical argumentation is not properly framed as it wrenches "an ethical problem out of its embedded context" and thus "severs the problem from its roots."[10] For example, if I were to see a homeless woman and her dog on the street, using Singer's line of reasoning I would ask whether giving the woman and her dog some money would prevent something bad from happening and whether I would be comparably harmed by the loss of the money. I would think it would in the former question and would not in the latter. So the ethical choice would be to give her whatever cash I had available. Perhaps, if an ATM were nearby, I might get her and her dog a little extra money.

But this way of thinking about the situation allows us to ignore larger questions: Is there a homeless shelter for the woman and her dog? Why are this woman and her canine companion homeless on the street in the first place? Is she here because the women's shelter doesn't accept dogs and she just can't leave her companion behind? What are the social and cultural forces that created this situation, and can my putting $20 into her hat really do any good or does it just make me feel like I'm acting heroically? Kheel argued that truncated narratives also set up a binary in which there is a victim and a hero, and thus obscure the possibility that the hero may be part of the cause of the larger problem.

As it is usually practiced, ethical theorizing detaches us from our actual moral experiences and practices through abstract reasoning. It sidesteps the complex social and political structures and ideologies that are always in play. It also sets aside our particular concerns, our relationships, and the other things that make life worth living. It thus can seem rather alienating, and an alienating theory will not help us to begin to solve the myriad problems that it is supposedly designed to help us address.

If moral requirements are such that our moral decisions and actions always detach us from those things that make our lives meaningful, then it is likely that most people will simply ignore moral requirements. Alienating moral theories would thus be self-defeating. If the goal of ethics is to help guide moral action, but the actions toward which individuals are guided are those that are contrary to leading satisfying, meaningful lives, then the theories will not in fact help guide action at all. Even if moral theory only guides us toward actions that occasionally force us to forego those things that are important in our lives, the problem remains.

There is another way in which traditional ethical theories may lead to a problematic form of alienation. Since ethical theories force us to focus on certain features of a situation in a narrow way, the narrow focus flattens or erases the complexity of actual moral problems. They, therefore, fail to capture all the richness of moral experience; they frame moral problems in ways that leave out some of what matters in the situation. This flattening or erasure thus alienates us from our environments, or at least important aspects of those environments. In doing so, it also alienates us from possible interpretations of the context in which we find ourselves—interpretations that could lead to an expanded understanding not only of the troubling situation, but also of one's role in it. When certain features of a situation are taken as given, when the background conditions that led to the moral problem are overlooked, certain potential solutions are obscured. The capacity for moral imagination itself becomes limited and this limitation may cause us to fail to see our way out of a moral problem. That moral theories might alienate us from possible solutions to moral problems would be a deeply troubling form of alienation, indeed.

One central component of our environments is our relationships with others—other humans, other animals, and the networks we form and that form us. Traditional ethical theories tend to ignore these centrally important relations, often positing that we are in the world as thinkers and actors without having come to learn how to think and act with the assistance of a community of thinkers and actors. This lack of contextualization leads to the bizarre idea that what we accomplish, we accomplish alone. Traditional theories tend to ignore or downplay not just the meaning of the relationships we are in, but the way those relationships shape who we are.

Insofar as traditional ethical theories alienate people from the moral problems we are confronted with, and a rich understanding of the lives of those in need, and the people and other animals we love, and the communities and practices that are meaningful and valuable in our lives, and from the possibility of becoming more fully in tune with the rich and complicated world in which we live, they fail.

Traditional Ethical Theory and Animal Liberation

Sadly, much of the contemporary animal liberation movement continues to be guided by traditional ethical theories with their flaws. Consider the common arguments presented for going vegan—arguments that are influenced by Tom Regan's rights view or Peter Singer's consequentialism. These arguments, though coming from different traditions within ethics, share the idea that there is no morally relevant distinction between human and nonhuman animals that can be invoked to justify raising animals to be slaughtered for food.

Regan argues that we should not focus on the differences between humans and nonhumans but the similarities. Because both humans and nonhumans are individually experiencing subjects of a life who have an individual welfare that matters to them regardless of what others might think, there is no morally important difference between them and us. Subjects of a life "want and prefer things, believe and feel things, recall and expect things. And all these dimensions of our life, including our pleasure and our pain, our enjoyment and suffering, our satisfaction and frustration, our continued existence or our untimely death—all make a difference to the quality of our life as lived, as experienced, by us as individuals."[11] Since animals also have these experiences as subjects of a life, they too have a value that should be respected.

For Singer, because animals used for food are beings who can suffer and who have an interest in not suffering, we are no more justified in violating their interests than we are in violating the like interests of any being who has such interests. To confine, control, manipulate, transport, and ultimately slaughter animals for food in contexts in which there are other foods available is to disregard their morally important interests in ways that cannot be justified.[12] By carefully reasoning about the capacities that matter morally, being a subject-of-a-life in Regan's case or an individual who has interests and can suffer in Singer's case, and by documenting the ways that modern, industrial food production disrespects animals and violates their rights or interests, both conclude that veganism is the only morally justified option.

These are arguments that are often adopted by those within the animal liberation movement. Although they are quite powerful arguments, insofar as they are extensions of traditional ethical theories that now include other animals, they are nonetheless open to some of the same criticisms.

Dangers of Focusing on Sameness

Arguments that seek to "extend" the boundary of moral concern outward tend to focus on sameness. If a human is able to suffer and that is why we think it is wrong to needlessly cause that human to suffer (in the name of some cultural ritual, for instance), then if we want to be non-prejudicial, we shouldn't allow any being who can similarly suffer to be used in that ritual instead. And surely other animals feel pain the way we feel pain, so needlessly causing pain should be just as wrong.

And it's not just the ability to suffer that we share with other animals. Ethological and cognitive research shows that other animals share many of the qualities that we admire in ourselves and to which we attach moral significance, so we ought to admire and value those qualities in whatever bodies they arise. Many species of nonhumans have rich social relationships—orangutan mothers stay with their young for ten years and, even though they eventually part company, they continue to keep their relationships over time. Less solitary animals—such as chimpanzees, baboons, wolves, and elephants—maintain extended family units built upon complex individual relationships for long periods of time, in some cases up to fifty years. Meerkats in the Kalahari Desert are known to sacrifice their own safety by staying with sick or injured family members so that the fatally ill will not die alone.

Like humans, many nonhuman animals negotiate their social environments by being particularly attentive to the emotional states of others around them. When a conspecific is angry, it is a good idea to get out of his way. Animals that develop lifelong bonds are known to suffer deeply from the death of their partners and friends. Studies in cognitive ethology have suggested that some nonhumans engage in manipulative and deceptive activity, can construct "cognitive maps" for navigation, act altruistically, and appear to understand symbolic representation and use language.

So many, if not most, of the capacities that we like about ourselves have been observed, maybe in less elaborate form, in the nonhuman world.

I think that some of the work that has been undertaken to explore the ways we are like other animals and they are like us has been important and has led to new avenues of inquiry that help us rethink how we have conceptualized certain ideas and practices. One important example of the insights we gain from exploring similarities comes from looking at the ways that other animals follow norms.

A norm is a standard of social behavior that is expected by a group. When someone transgresses that norm there are usually noticeable, often unpleasant, consequences, depending on the context. For example, if the norm violator is a new member of a group, then the reaction to the violation is going to be different from the norm violator who is known as a "trouble-maker," particularly if it is a repeated violation. Most of the literature about social norms assumes that it is unique to humans, but it seems that the emotional structures that underlie norm governance exist in other animals who are similar to humans. It seems that these very structures developed to serve a social purpose and it is unlikely that closely related species facing similar social pressures would develop very different psychological mechanisms to address those pressures.

Chimpanzees are excellent examples. In natural settings where populations are not threatened, chimpanzees live in fission–fusion societies in which their smaller, tighter-knit groups of between four to ten come together with the larger community of approximately a hundred individuals on a fairly regular, although not day-to-day, basis. The ability to share resources, exchange information, and to manage social interactions in such a large group would best be facilitated through adherence to some set of norms. In addition, the complex behaviors exhibited in these regular meetings would also be best explained by the existence of norms.

Chimpanzees possess long-term memory; they are socially tolerant and intelligent; they have quite flexible social repertoires; they have complex communicative abilities (some can even can use basic human symbolic-language systems); they understand and respond to the emotions of others; they comprehend the consequences of their and others' actions; and there is at least some evidence that they are able to inhibit their behaviors. They also engage in complex behaviors that researchers have variously described as "fairness," "other-regarding behavior," "inequity tolerance," "punishment or sanction," "cooperation," and "retaliation." It is possible that this is the wrong way to describe the behaviors, but at least in some cases, norm-based descriptions do seem apt.

Here are a few of those cases.

In Bossou, in southeastern Guinea, West Africa, chimpanzees are occasionally observed crossing roads that intersect with their territories. One of the roads is busy with traffic, the other is mostly a pedestrian route; both are dangerous to the chimpanzees. Video recordings of the chimpanzees as they are about to cross show adult males taking up forward and rear positions and adult females and youngsters staying in the more protected middle. The positioning of dominant and bolder individuals, in particular the alpha male, was found to change depending on both the degree of risk and the number of adult males present. Researchers suggest that cooperative action in the higher-risk situation was probably aimed at maximizing group protection. This sort of risk-taking for the sake of others is also often observed in male patrols of territorial boundaries in other parts of Africa. In these instances, a bold male, who may or may not be the alpha of the group, together with others with whom he has an alliance, begin a patrol with the goal of potential food rewards as well as protecting the group from neighboring threats.[13]

Frans de Waal and Sarah Brosnan developed a series of tests in captivity, to try to analyze cooperative behavior in the form of food-sharing among chimpanzees. They found that adults were more likely to share food with individuals who had groomed them earlier in the day. They suggested that the results could be explained in two ways: the "good-mood hypothesis," in which individuals who have received grooming are in a benevolent mood and respond by sharing with all individuals; or the "exchange hypothesis," in which the individual who has been groomed responds by sharing food only with the groomer. The data indicate that the sharing was specific to the previous groomer. The chimpanzees remembered who had performed a service (grooming) and responded to that individual by sharing food.

Brosnan and de Waal also observed that grooming between individuals who rarely did so was found to have a greater effect on sharing than grooming between partners who commonly groomed. Among partnerships in which little grooming was usually exchanged, there was a more pronounced effect between those who groomed earlier on their subsequent food sharing. They suggest that being groomed by an individual who doesn't usually groom might be more noticeable and thus warrant greater response, whether in the form of food sharing or what Brosnan and de Waal call "calculated reciprocity." They write, "not only do the chimpanzees regulate their food sharing based on previous grooming, but they recognize unusual effort and reward accordingly."[14]

In a different set of studies, de Waal and his collaborators described reconciliation behaviors in which a high-ranking female worked to help two male chimpanzees "make up" after an altercation. This kind of behavior, in which the female first attends to the "winner," then reassures the "loser" and encourages him to follow her to a grooming session with the winner, has no obvious or immediate benefit for the female, but does impact social harmony. Once the males begin grooming each other, the female will usually leave them alone.[15]

I have a group of friends who are chimpanzees and their social interactions among one another, and sometimes with me, always give me a lot to think about. Here are a couple of examples. There's usually a lot of excitement when I visit, probably because it is something different and also because I bring lots of treats. Maybe they are even happy to see me! During one visit, Keeli, an adolescent male, started displaying in ways that are inappropriate for a chimpanzee in his position in the social hierarchy. At one point, Darrell, then the alpha male, decided it was time to put Keeli in his place and began displaying and chasing Keeli around the play yard, smacking him when he got close enough. While this was going on, the other chimpanzees in the group tried to get out of their way, which is quite typical. On this occasion, however, Sarah, the older female, began "woaow" distress vocalizations. Upon hearing the vocalizations, Darrell continued chasing Keeli around the enclosure but also began reassuring all the other chimpanzees as he did so. The reassurance not only calmed the other chimps down but also slightly distracted Darrell from the intensity of his pursuit. When he eventually caught Keeli, he smacked him, but not as hard as he might have done had he been in full pursuit. The next day, Keeli sat apart from the group pouting.

On another occasion, I observed a surprising set of behaviors that still has me scratching my head. Sarah likes to look at books, so when I visit I often bring her children's books that can withstand chimpanzee handling for at least a few minutes. I gave Sarah her book and before she could really start "reading" it, Harper, a young male, came over and took it away. Sarah didn't struggle with Harper when he took it. Then moments later, Sheba, a very smart female (the daughter of Nim Chimpsky), who didn't appear to me to have noticed Harper's behavior because she was happily eating the dried mangos I brought her, went over to Harper and took the book from him. This in itself wouldn't be surprising; taking things that others have is typical among members of a group who aren't clearly dominant. What was surprising was that rather than keeping the book for herself, Sheba promptly gave it back to Sarah. There were no vocalizations that I was aware of that might indicate Sarah was distressed by Harper's thievery nor that Sheba was trying to appease any distress. It just looked to me as though Sheba was setting things right.

How might we explain the risky behavior the males engage in to protect the group while it's crossing the road? Or the strategic exchange of food and grooming? Or the punishment and reconciliation behaviors after altercations? Or the rectification that Sheba engaged in? One plausible account would be that the chimpanzees are trying to promote social harmony or wellbeing (in addition to furthering their own) and that they achieve this, in part, by recognizing and acting on certain norms. In the case of the male protection of the group, there is coordinated activity that the strong engage in for the sake of the others. In the case of food exchange for grooming, individuals remember the behavior of others and reward it, particularly when longer-term positive social engagement is desired. The behaviors I observe among my chimpanzee friends may best be explained by seeing that the chimpanzees understand social norms, they distinguish right or apt or appropriate behavior from wrong or inappropriate behavior, and act to enforce the norms. I'm doubtful that these chimpanzees ask themselves whether they should be acting the way they are acting or whether their actions are justified, but I do think they are acting according to norms.

In light of these cases, one of the commonly used reasons for thinking that humans are separate from and superior to other animals—the idea that we are norm-governed and that other animals just act on their immediate desires—starts to look rather weak. And showing how these human-exceptionalist arguments are flawed is important to overcoming prejudices. But although the recognition of similarities between us and other animals helps to break down the divisions that have long separated humans from all the other animals, looking for ways that other animals are like us may reinforce anthropocentrism.

I often distinguish two senses of anthropocentrism. The first is what I think of as *inevitable* anthropocentrism. We are humans and our perceptions are necessarily human. I see things from my perspective and you see things from your perspective, and these are distinct human perspectives. They may be mine and yours, but they're human perspectives nonetheless. That we experience the world from a human perspective doesn't mean that we can't work to see things from the perspectives of nonhumans, and I'll argue that empathy is a skill that helps us in doing this.

The second sort of anthropocentrism is an *arrogant* anthropocentrism. It is a type of human chauvinism that not only locates humans at the center of everything, but elevates the human perspective above all others. A focus on similarities can provide openings for thinking about ourselves, our practices, and our concepts in new ways, but we also run the risk of unwittingly projecting our human preoccupations onto other animals and engaging in arrogant anthropocentrism. Insofar as Regan and Singer are perpetuating a type of unwitting but nonetheless pernicious form of anthropocentrism through their extensionist arguments, they may be undermining the goals they are trying to reach.

Though I tend to agree with Regan and Singer's general conclusions, I think there are better ways to get to them, as you will see in the chapters ahead. The standard arguments in animal ethics follow traditional approaches in relying on abstract individualism, where individual interests and experiences are put into categories of similarity, generalized over, and become interchangeable. Of course, both Regan and Singer would acknowledge that individual suffering and experiences are unique to the individual who has them, but from the ethical point of view they can be detached from the individual and the community of friends and kin with whom the individual lives. What ends up mattering then is the harm or interest setback, the suffering or disrespect, understood *abstractly*. To recapitulate: the harm or interest setback matters, but it does so in the context of a *particular* life. The abstract perspective allows us to overlook what is important from the other's point of view, and it also obscures the unique capacities that other animals possess and might be valued in themselves. Too often in this abstraction, we substitute our own judgments of what is beneficial for other animals for what may in fact promote their wellbeing.

Because animal ethics has tended to emerge from or extend traditional approaches to ethics, the arguments used to promote animal liberation or animal rights focus on individuals in isolation from the larger political and social structures of power that undergird the domination of animals as well as oppression based on race, class, gender, ability, and sexuality, among other things. Focusing on the wider contexts as well as the differences *and* similarities between individuals within those contexts will assist us in getting to the roots of the problems that animal ethics is designed to help us solve.

Moving Beyond Principle-based Ethics

Rather than abandoning ethics in response to the limitations I just mentioned, we might theorize in a way that recognizes that our moral experiences are so diverse and so complex that they cannot be reduced to abstractions. In ethics, this position is sometimes called "particularism" and it rejects overarching, codifiable ethical theories that try to produce principles to direct and motivate right action. Some have suggested that it is an illusion that there can ever be an abstract theory that will be applicable in every similar context. There are always too many important differences that should be attended to but that end up being relegated to the background in an attempt to employ abstract theory.

These abstract theories are alienating, too; the judgments that usher from them work from the outside in, rather than from the inside out. In order to act rightly, a moral agent must submit herself to the authority of external forces or internalized impersonal norms that originated externally and, in doing this, she is detaching herself from her commitments, personality, or as philosopher and novelist Iris Murdoch put it, her own "total vision of life."

Murdoch's criticism of ethical theory is particularly potent. She compares morality to shopping—the ethical agent enters the shop "in a condition of totally responsible freedom" and surveys the products and chooses to purchase one product or another. Shopping is public, and one understands the shopper through his choices and actions, much as the modern economist understands the preference satisfaction of Economic Man through his choices and actions. The inner life of the shopper, of Economic Man, and of the moral agent understood through traditional ethical theory is "parasitic" on his outward behaviors.[16] These outward behaviors become the focal point of ethical choice and action, and the inner life of the agent remains mysterious or, when accessible, beside the point of ethical theorizing.

But the inner life is not only important; it is inextricable from the action that springs from it. The richness of moral experience can't be stripped down to abstract reason. As Murdoch suggests, a more balanced and more accurate account of moral experiences would include an analysis of the process and work of *attending* to a problem:

> [I]f we consider what the work of attention is like, how continuously it goes on, and how imperceptibly it builds up structures of value round about us, we shall not be surprised that at crucial moments of choice most of the business of choosing is already over. . . . The moral life, on this view, is something that goes on continually, not something that is switched off in between the occurrence of explicit moral choices. What happens in between such choices is indeed what is crucial.[17]

In order to provide a full account of what moral decisions involve, an account that would include what goes on between choices, a more robust picture of both the inner workings of the agent and the outer "structures of value round about us" must be painted.

There are (at least) two ways to work to provide this fuller account. The first is to pay attention to context; the second is to develop our "attention" or "care."[18] When taken together, contextualism and caring perception allow us to paint a more accurate picture of our moral experiences, decisions, and actions. Let me briefly mention why contextualization is important before turning to my main focus on caring perception—what I will ultimately call *entangled empathy*.

Attention to context is not a prominent feature of contemporary ethical theory or in discussions regarding animal liberation wherein, more often than not, abstractions reign. This failure to attend to context is not merely an oversight, because a focus on principles necessarily obscures context. Principle-based theories deny the ways that context shapes reasons, values, and choices. For example, breaking a law may provide a reason against an action in some contexts, but may not count as a reason at all in other contexts. Consider a case of stealing someone's property. The law provides a reason not to do so. However, if one cannot afford food or medication for one's loved one, the fact that stealing is against the law does not count as a reason for not taking action. Or if the "property" in question is another animal (say a dog chained to a fence who is not fed and has no water), then rescuing the dog, which currently amounts to stealing someone's property, may be the right thing to do.

A principle-based theory that holds that one ought always

to follow the law cannot make sense of these cases. Of course, what the law says and what an ethical theory may require is not always the same thing. There are numerous examples of unethical laws. The point here is simply that principles that are meant to provide reasons are not always going to do so when contexts change. For any principle one examines, there will be examples of contexts in which that principle doesn't provide reasons for action at all, or provides reasons for a contrary action. A reason for acting in one case may not count for a reason in all cases.

In addition, reasons, values, choices, and the actions that follow from them cannot be properly analyzed in isolation from the context in which they operate—a context that includes the agent's other beliefs, desires, reasons, and values, as well as the larger social structures that shape beliefs and desires and facilitate or hinder choices and actions. A proper analysis of the larger context in which we exercise our moral agency cannot be done by an appeal to how the various parts of the whole fit together under a principle-based description of how best to understand the context. Rather, what is required is the right kind of attentiveness to the context and the right moral perception. But what is the right kind of attentiveness or moral perception?

Ethics of Care

I will argue that the right kind of attentiveness is entangled empathy. However, we need to lay more groundwork before introducing that argument, both to get clearer about what the differences in approaches to ethical thinking amount to, and to situate my view in its historical context, since entangled empathy can be considered a part of the care tradition. I also want to try to clarify some misconceptions about the ethics of care to pay tribute to an important ethical perspective that has not been given its due.

The ethics of care first emerged when Carol Gilligan, a psychologist, and Nel Noddings, a philosopher of education, reacted to some of the research that was being conducted on moral development. Gilligan's work in particular was critical of the writings of Lawrence Kohlberg, a prominent psychologist who drew extensively on traditional ethical theories to identify types of moral reasoning. Kohlberg presented seventy young male students (ages 10–16) with a moral problem, known as the "Heinz Dilemma," which goes something like this:

> Mr. Heinz's wife was dying from a particular type of cancer. Doctors said a new drug might save her. The drug had been discovered by a local pharmacist who was charging ten times the money it cost to make the drug. This was much more than Heinz could afford.
>
> Heinz could only raise half the money, even after he received money from friends, family, and neighbors. He tried to work out a payment plan with the pharmacists who refused to sell it for a cheaper price or provide payment options. Heinz, desperate to save his wife, broke into the pharmacy and stole the drug.

Kohlberg then asked the young boys if they thought what Heinz did was right or not.

There were a range of answers, including: "Heinz was wrong because it's against the law to steal," which Kohlberg characterized as an early stage of *preconventional* moral development, where ethics is located in some external authority; "Heinz should have stolen it because a husband shouldn't let his wife die without doing anything," which Kohlberg characterized as a stage of *conventional* moral reasoning where ethics is being good and conforming to familial and social expectations; and "life is more valuable than property," which was characterized as *postconventional* morality and involves abstract reasoning.

In all, Kohlberg identified six distinct stages. In Stage 1, the students think doing the right thing is obeying authority. During Stage 2, they are no longer so impressed by any one authority, and try to figure out ways to work between authorities. In Stage 3, they think doing what is right is being helpful to family and friends. During Stage 4, they are focused on social order. During the final two Stages, 5 and 6, students become interested in acting according to certain principles. At Stage 5, they might be concerned with "rights" or "fairness," and at the highest stage they think in terms of universal principles.[19]

Gilligan took issue with Kohlberg's conclusions, his methodology, and his focus on the moral development of boys. The publication of her book *In a Different Voice* provided the theoretical and empirical grounding for what came to be called "an ethics of care," which was an alternative to "the ethics of justice." Gilligan proposed a different scale that did not see detached abstraction as the apex of moral development. Her view focused more on connection, relationships, and nonviolence. The division between justice and care, to a large extent, paralleled the different sorts of responses to ethical issues that tracked gender socialization, where girls, even in early play experiences, are often steered toward more caring and collaborative roles and boys toward more hierarchical and rule-based roles. Girls often responded to ethical questions by asking further questions about larger social relationships, whereas boys often responded by invoking social standards or rules. An ethics of care sometimes was associated with "feminine" characteristics and an ethics of justice "masculine" ones.

This association was unfortunate because it further entrenched stereotypical gender roles and seemed to preclude the idea that men are caring. It also led people to dismiss an ethics of care as a "woman's ethic." An ethics of care focuses on the particularity of caring relationships, informed by difference in context, as well as the racial, economic, ethnic, cultural, and differently gendered experiences of individuals and those they care for. It's a theory for all people and is an important tool for us to think about our relationships beyond humans. That the theory was developed by women as an alternative to what look like detached, alienating theories, in a social context in which gender is assumed to be binary, may have lent a certain insight to the theory. Nonetheless, it isn't a "feminine" theory or a "woman's ethic." An ethics of care provides remedies for some of the failures I have mentioned above. Here is a quick look at the differences in emphasis between more traditional ethical approaches and the alternative that care theory provides.

1. Abstraction vs. Context

As I have been discussing, in traditional ethical theories ethical claims are not designed to fit the specifics of each individual situation. The details and particularities of the situation must be abstracted away so that what remains is the rule or principle. The traditional approach claims that when one is able to reason impartially from abstract principles one has achieved the highest level of moral development. In contrast, an ethics of care finds the details that make up a situation to be indispensable to an adequate resolution of any moral problem. It makes being reflective about context a crucial part of moral experiences.

2. Individualism vs. Relationality

Traditional theories focus on a conception of the rational "man" without any reference to even the most basic and necessary relationships among people. The nature of morality in this picture springs from the universal capacity of individuals to reason, rather than from the connections individuals have with one another. Care theorists view people as embedded in and emerging from social relationships.

3. Impartiality vs. Connection

Impartial reasoning is the highest form of ethical deliberation in the traditional approaches. For a decision to be just and unbiased, it must be impartial, and detached from personal and emotional responses to a situation. An ethics of care rejects the kind of impartiality that requires moral decision-makers to detach themselves from the context in which they are making decisions, including who they are, the nature of their relationships with others in the situation, and their own involvement in that situation. Care ethicists deny that a decision-maker who remains situated will necessarily make a more biased decision than one who pretends that he or she can separate from the situation.

4. Conflict vs. Responsiveness

Most traditional theories focus on situations of conflict and choice. An ethics of care has to address situations of conflict of course, but it is also concerned with how people come to see a moral problem as a problem in the first place and tries to explore the moral imagination, not only as a way to reframe problems but as a means to move toward solutions.

The justice/care debate, even as I have just presented it, seems to involve a set of binaries, and there have certainly been proponents of justice or care that see themselves as opposed to the other. But justice and care needn't be at odds, and most contemporary care theorists recognize that connection and concern are matters of both care and of justice. Importantly, reason and emotion cannot meaningfully be separated either, as they are mutually informing. Any compelling moral theory has to recognize that cognition/reason and affect/emotion cannot be disentangled. Rather than generating distance between us and them, justice and care, we need a theory that bridges perceived gaps between reason/emotion or self/other by recognizing the ways that each side of the bridge shapes the other without collapsing into it.

The Feminist Care Tradition in Animal Ethics

The Feminist Care Tradition in Animal Ethics is the term that Carol J. Adams and Josephine Donovan use to describe work that has been going on for almost as long as the traditional approaches to animal ethics, but has not received the sort of attention it deserves.[20] This is ironic because "attention" is one of the central features of care ethics. Within the feminist care tradition in animal ethics, attention is directed to individual animals of course, but also to the differences between animals, as well as to the larger structural forces that separate and maintain distance between us and them.

There are all sorts of differences between humans and other animals; we are different one from the other as members of biological groups and as individuals. Chimpanzees are closer to humans genetically and evolutionarily than either is to another great ape, the gorilla. All great apes are different from ungulates; carnivores are quite distinct from herbivores; monotremes are very unlike cats. Given the tremendous variety of animal shapes, sizes, social structures, behaviors, and habitats, separating humans from all other animals is a peculiar way to categorize organisms. Just as the category "disabled," the category "animal" is too vast and too vague, and we would be wise to focus on as much particularity as we can.

The traditional approaches to animal ethics, as I mentioned, tend to ignore these differences and focus on similarities in order to extend the sphere of moral consideration outward. Debates among feminists highlight just how damaging overlooking difference can be. Thinking that all "women" are alike or experience the world in the same ways assimilates women into a white, heterosexual, cis-gendered, able body, and obscures the very real ways in which different axes of domination impact women differently. These insights are important for the feminist care tradition in animal ethics, too. When we are searching for sameness—how we might share the same general type of intelligence or cognitive skills, the same sensitivities and vulnerabilities, the same emotional responses—we might obscure or overlook distinctively valuable aspects of the lives of others. When we assimilate other animals into our human-oriented framework, we grant them consideration in virtue of what we believe they share with us; we allow them to be seen through our distinctively human gaze. And in our magnanimous embrace of the other, we end up occluding an important part of what makes them, them.

The feminist care tradition in animal ethics urges us to attend to other animals in all of their difference, including differences in power within systems of human dominance in which other animals are seen and used as resources or tools. So another way that the care tradition differs from traditional approaches is through its analysis of the economic, political, racial, gendered, and cultural underpinnings of systems of animal exploitation, commodification, and cruelty. By analyzing the specific contexts in which systems of power operate, the feminist care tradition is concerned with justice, as it is within these larger structures that injustice emerges and is reinforced.

Within the care tradition in animal ethics, compassion, sympathy, and empathy are the focus of much discussion. Although some people refer to these as "moral emotions," they are more appropriately thought of as different forms of attention. Constructive connections exist among these forms of attention and there are differences as well. Sympathy, as I discuss in the next chapter, is a more detached attitude toward the other and is elicited only in conditions of distress. Moral attention in response to distress or tragedy is often referred to as compassion, and that is part of the reason I think entangled empathy is preferable for helping us think through those complex relations that involve more than suffering. Compassion has a rich history in East Asian thought, and as Deane Curtin has recently written it is quite similar to the entangled empathy I discuss in this book.[21] All of these forms of moral attention recognize that reason cannot be isolated from embodied emotional experiences and thus provide important tools for rethinking our relationships. ❖

BEFORE DISCUSSING ENTANGLED empathy, I want to explore the variety of ways that empathy is understood. Even though empathy is a fairly new concept, it has generated a lot of contentious debate. In this chapter I will discuss different types of empathy and explore some of the disagreements that have accompanied it. In the process, I hope to make clear how I understand it. Empathy is a particular type of attention, what I think of as a kind of moral perception. Moral perception is not the same as ordinary sense perception, in that the latter doesn't often require reflection and correction, whereas moral perception does. Both types of perception aren't just interior processes; often, in order to perceive accurately, we need to reflect in light of information.

Look at this drawing of an attentive duck.

When I tell you that this is a "reversible figure," in which you can discern the image in two different ways, your perception may change. You might remember the famous rabbit–duck optical illusion and then see the rabbit. If you've never heard of this experiment, you might see the rabbit when I mention that the duck's beak is her ears. Having more information and then reflecting on the image will help you to perceive more accurately. You may have perceived the rabbit first, unaware that there was also a duck present; in either case, more information and reflection on that information can help you to distinguish the image better. You may be like me and have to tell yourself there is a rabbit in order to see the rabbit, and a duck to see the duck.

Unlike ordinary sense perception, moral perception can occur in a purely narrative or discursive context. Consider both the narrator's perceptual shift and your own in this example of a Sunday morning subway ride in New York:

> People were sitting quietly—some reading newspapers, some lost in thought, some resting with their eyes closed. It was a calm, peaceful scene.
>
> Then suddenly, a man and his children entered the subway car. The children were so loud and rambunctious that instantly the whole climate changed.
>
> The man sat down next to me and closed his eyes, apparently oblivious to the situation. The children were yelling back and forth, throwing things, even grabbing people's papers. It was very

disturbing. And yet, the man sitting next to me did nothing.

It was difficult not to feel irritated. I could not believe that he could be so insensitive as to let his children run wild like that and do nothing about it, taking no responsibility at all. It was easy to see that everyone else on the subway felt irritated, too. So finally, with what I felt was unusual patience and restraint, I turned to him and said, "Sir, your children are really disturbing a lot of people. I wonder if you couldn't control them a little more?"

The man lifted his gaze as if to come to a consciousness of the situation for the first time and said softly, "Oh, you're right. I guess I should do something about it. We just came from the hospital where their mother died about an hour ago. I don't know what to think, and I guess they don't know how to handle it either."[22]

Having more information and reflecting on the context, one's irritation dissolves. In fact, most people would find it callous, perhaps cruel, to keep being annoyed in the face of learning this poor father's news. The information of the tragedy that befell him and his children alters what is salient about the situation. Loud, disruptive, rambunctious children who just lost their mother are much easier to tolerate than those who are simply badly brought up. And a father who just lost his partner not currently paying attention to the behavior of their children is understandable. The very same actions described differently are perceived differently.

Moral perception requires a sensitive responsiveness to a wide array of information and that requires an exercise of judgment: to determine what information is available, what additional information might be required, and whether the information that one acquires is relevant. These exercises of judgment are different from exercises of moral judgment, as traditionally understood through the ethical theories discussed in the last chapter. Moral judgment, for example, typically involves a process that addresses how, when, and whether to apply a moral principle, or whether one's intentions are the appropriate ones, or how much good over bad will arise as a result of the actions that spring from the judgment. Moral judgments typically don't involve reflection on how the situation arose that is requiring the judgment (and they often explicitly claim that the situation is beside the point, as I mentioned). Nor do they ask whether the description used to assess the situation is fitting or accurate.

Moral perception is prior to these kinds of judgments. Moral perception helps a person to see what is morally relevant or important in a particular context. I want to suggest that empathetic moral perception guides us to perceive a situation more accurately; it may also help shape our judgments and allow us to do the right thing in light of what we perceive. I'll be talking more about this. However, before I do, I want to distinguish various kinds of empathy and to see how they are different from other ways of caring.

Sympathy and Empathy

The use of the term *empathy* is relatively new, just over a hundred years old. The first systematic analysis of empathy is often linked to Theodor Lipps's theory of *Einfühlung*. Writing in the early 1900s, Lipps suggested that empathy was a specific perceptual way of understanding the world and others in it. Some philosophers took up the idea of empathy and it quickly became a term that referred to a variety of experiences that were of interest to psychologists. In the last decade or so, empathy has gained increasing attention in ethics and in the last few years has been discussed in greater detail in animal ethics. Nonetheless, both the concept of empathy and the actual phenomenon have been understood in many different, often contradictory, ways.

Some of the ways that empathy is currently understood include:

- The ability to put oneself into the shoes of another person to understand her emotions and feelings (a form of inner imitation or simulation)
- A form of psychological inference in which observation, memory, knowledge, and reasoning are combined to yield insights into the thoughts and feelings of others
- An emotional response more appropriate to someone else's situation than to one's own
- An other-oriented emotional response congruent with the other's perceived welfare
- An emotional response that stems from the

> apprehension of another's emotional state and that
> is similar to what the other person is feeling or
> would be expected to feel in that situation.[23]

And in everyday use, empathy is often thought of as connected with sympathy.

However, there are important differences between sympathy and empathy. As I understand it, sympathy is a response to something bad, untoward, unfortunate, or unpleasant happening to someone else in which the individual sympathizing retains all of her attitudes, beliefs, feelings, etc. When a lost child cries out in fear, a sympathetic observer will recognize the fear and attempt to comfort the child. When a stray cat is meowing at the door, the sympathetic human will offer food and perhaps shelter. When an elderly person slips as she attempts to enter the elevator, a sympathetic person will hold the elevator and help the person enter. In all cases of sympathetic engagement with a distressed other, the sympathizer does not try to understand or feel what the child, or the cat, or the elderly person feels from their point of view. There is usually no feeling with the other. Rather, the sympathizer identifies the unpleasant or unfortunate event as unpleasant or unfortunate for the individual experiencing it, but does not experience it herself.

Sympathy involves maintaining one's own attitudes and adding to them a concern for another. Sympathy for another is felt from the outside, the third-person perspective. I can feel sympathy for another's plight, even pity, but remain rather removed from that plight. For example, I might think

"Oh, isn't that a shame!" when I see a hungry homeless woman and her puppy on a leash, but nonetheless walk away. And sympathy, as I am understanding it, more than empathy has the potential for being condescending. Because one attempts to keep one's own attitudes, beliefs, even prejudices distinct from the other, one can sympathize with another when sympathy isn't called for. For example, a person might observe some unusual or kinky behavior and, because the viewer might find it unpleasant, she might feel sympathy for the experient, even though the latter may actually be enjoying it. While we're being sympathetic, we attempt to be disconnected from others.

Empathy, however, recognizes connection with and understanding of the circumstances of the other. This understanding may not be complete and often is in need of revisions. However, the goal is to try to take in as much about another's situation and perspective as possible. And empathy has more "grip" than sympathy; it packs a greater motivational punch, as it were. Empathy does not involve abandoning one's own attitudes, perspectives, and commitments. It provides an important reference point from which to assess the features of a situation and to ask appropriate questions. Empathetic attunement or perception is directed toward the wellbeing of another. In these ways, empathy remedies the deficits of traditional ethical theories that miss or distort the important parts of moral experience as I discussed in the last chapter.

Different Forms of Empathy

We empathize in different ways at different times. One

form of empathy that many different types of animals share involves emotional contagion or affective resonance. This is a spontaneous, somewhat reflexive, response to the feelings of another. Anyone who has lived with dogs will be familiar with this phenomenon. Dogs are emotional sponges—they often become stressed when their person is stressed, sad when their person is sad, joyful when their person is joyful.[24] I know if I start walking with a little spring in my step, my canine companions perk up, too. Infants and small children also regularly engage in these spontaneous reactions. This sort of reaction is referred to as "emotional contagion" or "affective resonance." It is a kind of embodied response to another individual or individuals in one's immediate environment and does not require any reflection or conceptualization or even understanding. This very basic type of empathy involves the direct perception of the emotions of others and automatically triggers or "activates the same emotion in the perceiver, without any intervening labeling, associative, or cognitive perspective-taking processes."[25] In the majority of cases, this initial response seems unavoidable.

Yawning is one of the most common examples of empathy as emotional contagion. If you see someone yawning, the chances are very high that you will unconsciously yawn yourself. Reports have been published that domestic dogs will yawn when their people yawn. In the last couple of years, studies have found that bonobos, chimpanzees, and some baboons, as well as wolves and parrots, yawn when they see others do the same.[26]

Typically, emotional contagion happens in the company

of familiar others. Different forms of empathy occur when those we are empathizing with are not immediately present. It seems this type of empathy only occurs in humans, rather than other animals. At an early age, children develop what has been described as "storied empathy."[27] Children often identify with the characters in stories and when the narrative indicates that the characters are suffering or scared or successful the child will empathize with the character, and that character is often not human. Storied empathy seems to suggest that we can empathize with non-existing beings, but what is really happening is that a fixed character with specific interests and needs faces very particular obstacles, and it is in that context in which empathy occurs. When a child understands that this storied character is fictional, the empathy experienced for that character fades.

Another form of empathy that is more cognitively engaging than emotional contagion but not as robust as the type of empathy that is relevant to ethical perception is sometimes referred to in the psychological literature as "primary" or "personal empathy." Here, the empathetic individual is able to connect their feelings to the reality of the individual being empathized with. At this stage, personal empathy allows one to empathize with the actual situation of another but does not distinguish one's own perspective from the perspective of the other. This is the type of empathy wherein an individual really puts herself in the shoes of the other and loses sight of herself. Empathy that exclusively involves this sort of "fellow feeling," in which the person empathizing loses herself in the emotions of another, doesn't allow much room for reflection and correction.

Similarly, just as one might lose oneself in empathizing with another, there is another type of empathy where the empathizer is unable to distinguish his or her own feelings or mental states more generally from those of another. This type of empathy is a form of projection and some theorists have limited their understanding of empathy to just these sorts of cases. They then claim that empathy is really a kind of narcissism and thus shouldn't play a role in reflective ethical engagement.

However, those of us, humans and maybe nonhumans, who have certain kinds of cognitive capacities, such as the ability to differentiate between self and other, can purposely and thoughtfully take the perspective of another being. In doing this, we can experience a different form of empathy. The primary difference between other forms of empathy and what has been called "cognitive empathy" is that in the latter the empathizer is not mirroring or projecting onto the emotions of the one being empathized with, but is engaged in a reflective act of imagination that puts her into the object's situation and/or frame of mind, and allows her to take the perspective of the other.

Consider what has now become an often-cited anecdotal report of a bonobo engaged in what Frans de Waal takes to be a form of cognitive empathy:

> Kuni, a female bonobo at the Twycross Zoo in England, once captured a starling. She took the bird outside and set it onto its feet, the right way up, where it stayed shaking. When the bird didn't

move, Kuni threw it a little, but it just fluttered. Kuni then picked up the starling, climbed to the highest point on the highest tree, and carefully unfolded the bird's wings, one wing in each hand, before throwing it into the air. When the bird still remained in the enclosure, Kuni guarded it for a long time against a curious juvenile.[28]

If Kuni is empathetically responding to the starling, her response is clearly different from the form of empathy in which she loses herself in the other. She is not shaking and is not described as being fearful, feelings the starling most likely is experiencing. Rather, she appears to be attentive to the needs or interests of the starling and may even believe that the starling would be better off flying away. She seems to distinguish herself from the starling, apparently recognizing that the starling flies on wings and she does not. Kuni doesn't jump with the bird off the highest branch. So she seems to be feeling with and reflecting on the state the starling is in at the same time. Once Kuni recognizes that the starling cannot fly away, she then protects the starling from danger.[29] Yet, if this is a form of cognitive empathy, it doesn't lead to the best outcome in terms of the wellbeing of the starling. Throwing a bird that cannot fly off the highest branch of the highest tree is not a particularly sophisticated act of empathy! More apt empathy would allow the empathizer to imagine more thoroughly the situation of the one with whom they are empathizing. Empathy of this sort enables the empathizer not only to grasp the other's state of mind or preferences or

49

interests, but to ascertain the features of the situation that affect her and information about what led to the object's being in that situation in the first place.

Being able to understand what another being feels, sees, and thinks, and to understand what they might need or desire, requires a fairly complex set of cognitive skills and emotional attunement. In their study of whether or not chimpanzees possess these capacities, referred to in this context as having a "theory of mind," Guy Woodruff and David Premack back in the 1970s devised a series of tests to try to determine whether chimpanzee Sarah was able to understand another's needs and help that other solve his problems.

Woodruff and Premack shot a series of videos that showed a human actor in a cage trying to obtain bananas that were inaccessible, or attempting to light a stove or change a light bulb. In each of the videos the solution to the particular problem was visually present. Sarah watched each video until the last five seconds, at which point the video was put on hold. Sarah was then presented with two photographs, only one of which was a solution to the problem the person in the video faced. The experimenter left the room and Sarah selected one of the two photographs by placing her selection in a designated location. Sarah made the correct selection in 21 of 24 trials. So it looked as though Sarah understood that the human actor was attempting to achieve a particular goal, understood that he faced a problem that he wanted to overcome, and was able to determine what would allow the actor to overcome the problem to reach his goal.

These tests weren't designed to determine whether

Sarah showed a high level of more advanced empathy. In fact, Woodruff and Premack thought of empathy as a purely emotional reaction and tried to control for it. But if we understand empathy as I have been suggesting we do— as the ability to blend emotion and cognition to understand the situation of the other and try to help them overcome a problem they may face—then this experiment suggests that Sarah did engage in a form of engaged empathy, although she was selective about it. It turns out that she picked the right responses to solve the problem for the actor who was played by a caregiver she liked, and chose the wrong responses or failed to solve the problem for the actor she didn't like as much. This suggests that she certainly was able to empathize with others, but only chose to do so with those she cared about.[30]

I think of empathy as a process. Although the process may not be linear, we can think of the various parts of the process as going something like this: The wellbeing of another grabs the empathizer's attention; then the empathizer reflectively imagines himself in the position of the other; and then he makes a judgment about how the conditions that the other finds herself in contribute to her state of mind or wellbeing. The empathizer will then carefully assess the situation and figure out what information is pertinent to empathize effectively with the being in question.

This sort of empathy doesn't separate emotion and cognition and will tend to lead to action because what draws our attention in the first place is another's experiential wellbeing. Once our perception starts the process, we will want to pay critical attention to the broader conditions that impact the wellbeing or flourishing of those with whom we are empathizing. This requires us to attend to things we might not have otherwise. Empathy of this sort requires gaining perspective and usually motivates the empathizer to act ethically.

In the psychological literature, empathy is often coupled with a motivational state in order for "helping action" to occur.[31] Generally, motivations fall into two mutually exclusive general categories: self-interested motivation and altruistic motivation.[32] Empathy that is more like emotional contagion is thought to be highly motivating, because one is experiencing something very similar to what the being empathized with is experiencing. If an animal is in pain in a trap, the one empathizing will move quickly to relieve both of their suffering. Cognitive empathy is thought to generate an altruistic motivation: when one is empathizing in this way one is trying to understand the perspective of the other, to feel the other's subjective experience, and to share her goals. To understand and feel what another is feeling and to embrace her goals is thought to involve motivation.

Recent discussions of how empathetic processes may have evolved in social animals as a capacity that aids in solving social problems suggest that both self-interested and other directed motivations may come "online" when one is empathizing with another. Social cognition is "expensive" in the sense that it requires a larger brain, which requires a lot of energy. It would be odd, from an evolutionary perspective, to have such a resource-intensive capacity emerge that didn't drive behavior.[33]

Nonetheless, we need to be careful about thinking of motivations in a dichotomous and exclusive way. The contrast between self-interested and other-directed or altruistic motivations, while clearly distinguishable in the extremes, may be hard to differentiate in a great majority of cases. Is a parent's motivation to help her child succeed self-regarding or other directed? It seems that an adequate answer would be both. In the next chapter I discuss a way of understanding the self as relational that challenges this dichotomous construction of motivation. Some people moved to help a distressed individual with whom they are empathizing may be motivated to end the distress because it causes them discomfort; others may be moved because they are unable to imagine themselves in a situation in need in which others do not come to their aid; some may be motivated because their sense of themselves as an empathetic person requires it; still others may be moved by more purely "altruistic" motivations. And some combination of motivations may be operating much of the time.[34]

Questioning Empathy's Role in Ethics

Some people are raising questions about what role, if any, empathy should play in ethics. Does one have to be empathetic in order to be ethical? Is empathy the best, only, or primary motivation for moral action? Is empathy needed prior to making moral judgments? Lately, some scholars have reacted very negatively to the increased attention to empathy in ethics. Paul Bloom, a psychologist at Yale, and Jesse Prinz, a philosopher at CUNY, both argue against empathy in their scholarship and in the popular press.[35] These empathy skeptics claim that research shows that when we think about inequality, for example, empathy is not particularly helpful, because it is biased and is not the best way to respond ethically. They suggest that emotions such as outrage, anger, or indignation (emotions that are, interestingly, usually associated with masculinity) may be more appropriate.

Skeptics about empathy tend to focus on controlled laboratory studies that show that empathy skews our moral judgments. I discuss the ways that entangled empathy can go wrong in Chapter 4 and how we can improve our empathetic skills. Here, however, I want to explore briefly a few of the biases that empathy is allegedly prone to. Of particular concern are what are called "in-group biases" and "proximity effects."[36]

The empathy skeptics are worried that empathy is more often directed to those who are like us, who are in our group, presumably members of our own species. This would certainly be a concern for me. They point to a few studies in which, for example, people are shown pictures of faces and their empathetic responses are measured. In some of those studies the subjects are found to empathize more with those who are from the same ethnic group. Skeptics admit that there are studies that don't show this bias. Indeed, I have read studies in which empathy was tested by showing images of animals who were being harmed. Not only did test subjects respond empathetically to the animals, but many commented that they wanted to try to help prevent the harm.[37] I suspect there are studies that will support any number of views on empathy's role in ethics. As Simon Baron-Cohen, a leading empathy researcher, puts it, "I am not convinced any lab studies correspond to real-world behavior." And given that all of us have witnessed people showing great empathy for others who are quite different from themselves, including nonhuman animals, it is at least possible that empathy is not limited to those like us.[38]

Another reason that skeptics want to reject empathy's role in ethics is that empathy tends to be selectively elicited for those who are close by and this can distort the proper ethical response to tragedy or misfortune. Prinz describes the significant outpouring of empathetic response for the victims of Hurricane Katrina in the United States. The conversation about the tragedy continued for a long time after the levies broke. He tells us the death toll was 1,836. He then reminds us that the year before Katrina the tsunami that hit Indonesia had a death toll of 315,000 and the response wasn't as strong. But Baron-Cohen uses the response to the tsunami as evidence that we don't have to be close to respond empathetically to the suffering of others. He tells us that "charitable donations flooded in from countries from around the world," and notes that "when we send $100 to a charity in Southeast Asia, we have no expectation or desire that it will ever be reciprocated. We just want to help."

Bloom writes that, "Each day, more than ten times the number of people who died in Hurricane Katrina die because of preventable diseases, and more than thirteen times as many perish from malnutrition." The conclusion the skeptics draw is that empathy is of no use in addressing these pressing ethical concerns. As Bloom observes, "The crucial question is not whose suffering touches us most but who needs us most." Of course, we are reliant on information we have access to, and we are only liable to hear about faraway tragedies, if we are already predisposed to find out how we might help those in need, or if we know people who live in those places, and/ or if the news media inform us. Once the information is available, I see no reason why empathy is any less effective at attending to the wellbeing of others as ethical theories that rely on reasoned deliberation or anger.

Although I think it is instructive to explore criticisms, the skeptics I have briefly discussed here direct their criticism at a type of empathy that is akin to an initial reaction, one that isn't subject to critical reflection. The empathy they have in mind is not quite emotional contagion, as it allows for some imaginative capacity, but it is an unreflective empathy. Entangled empathy, in contrast, directs our attention to the things that need moral response, can help provide context and understanding about what the right response would be, and, as we'll see in the next chapter, can provide us with a more accurate picture of who we are and what our responsibilities to others might be. Before turning to this discussion, I want to address one more serious misconception.

A Common Misconception about Empathy: Projection
One criticism I have heard a number of times about empathy, and to which I already briefly alluded in the discussion above, is that empathy can be reduced to a kind of "narcissistic projection" of our own interests and desires onto others, particularly nonverbal others. This is a serious concern in

animal-protection work where the desires that humans have about the wellbeing of nonhumans often gets substituted for their actual wellbeing. These desires come in two forms: *direct* desires, when we think another animal is lonely or sad or afraid, when in fact it is we who are feeling lonely or sad or imagine the animal will be afraid; and *mediated* desires, desires that stem from ideological commitments that are then projected onto animals.

With these two forms of desires come two forms of projection. The first is very familiar. Those of us who live with animals or work directly with them usually know a lot about the animals we spend time with, but we also have to keep an eye on our projections. As I've mentioned, since dogs are so prone to pick up our emotions, it is likely that projection can turn into a cycle. For instance, I might feel scared about taking Fuzzy, my rescued greyhound, to the veterinarian, and then Fuzzy, picking up on my fear, gets frightened. Once we arrive, I suggest to the vet that I have to stay with Fuzzy as he is too afraid. The veterinarian, picking up on my anxiety, thinks it would be better if Fuzzy wasn't with me during the examination.

Another example might be that I see a sick hen and believe she wants to be cuddled. I might sincerely feel that I can detect how much she wants to be cuddled, but what is really happening is that I'm accurately picking up on her feeling sick but then projecting my own wish to be cuddled when I'm sick onto her In this circumstance, the sick hen might be better off left alone, because contact with scary mammals stresses chickens out further rather than making them feeling comforted.[39]

An audience member at a conference at Hunter College once asked Peter Singer whether or not we should stop predation to eliminate animal suffering. Although he responded that he thought human interference had led to more harm than good, Singer replied that he would want to stop chimpanzees from fighting, if it could be done. Anyone who has witnessed chimpanzee altercations cannot help but respond with fear at the awesome violence they sometimes engage in. But fighting among chimpanzees is centrally important to their social interactions. It allows them to establish or reestablish their social hierarchy and, once the fighting is over, to engage in reconciliation, which strengthens social bonds. Stopping chimpanzees from ordinary fighting and altercations (with the possible exception of fatal conflicts) would actually be contrary to their interests and represents a form of projection and thus a failure of empathy. I was able to communicate this to Singer and I don't think he'll make this mistake again.

Mediated projection can also deeply affect the wellbeing of others. I was involved in a case many years ago wherein I saw firsthand just how harmful this sort of projection can be. An animal-protection organization with strong ideological commitments against any "use" of animals were supporting an animal refuge that held hundreds of animals, including over sixty chimpanzees. The organization refused to provide enrichment for the primates because they believed that human interference with wild animals was bad for the animals. Being left alone with as little human interaction as possible was what they thought would promote the animals' wellbeing and constituted a form of respect for them.

This refuge received nine enculturated chimpanzees who had worked in cognition research and were raised to rely on humans to provide them with not just food and water but with emotional and intellectual stimulation, as well as help in organizing their social lives. The refuge maintained its commitment to minimal human involvement to the detriment of the chimpanzees. The chimpanzees suffered terribly from this neglect: two of the older females stopped eating, and two of the males died. Before further tragedy could occur the chimpanzees were moved to a facility that could provide for their specific needs, and the remaining chimpanzees are now thriving.

The refuge's commitment to absolute principle caused them to project their views onto the animals. I find it hard to imagine how this could have happened. How do you look into the eyes of a chimpanzee in a barren cage with a cement floor, rocking herself for comfort, and not empathize and thus try to figure out what to do to ease her distress? I imagine the only way to hold onto a commitment to noninterference in the midst of obvious distress is to not pay attention, to look away, or to focus on the abstract principle rather than the particular experiences of an individual's suffering.[40]

Even when individuals are genuinely attempting to take the perspective of another—when they are mindful of the dangers of substituting their own frame of reference; their own interests, desires, or beliefs about what is good for the other; or ideological commitments about the good for those with whom they are empathizing—the possibility always remains that they have not adequately understood the other.

This is true among human beings as well as between humans and other animals. Who hasn't misread a situation with a friend or lover, a family member or neighbor, with all manner of disappointing, perhaps disastrous, results? Often in these circumstances we not only fail to understand the perspective of the other but forget that we should try harder to understand what they may be hearing, seeing, feeling, and thinking.

To avoid this sort of projection and the denial of the other that comes with it, and in order to genuinely empathize, the empathizer has to focus carefully on and take account of the specific context of the other, their idiosyncratic desires and personality, and the processes that shaped who they are. They would also have to recognize the other's developmental and, in the case of non-sentient beings, their ecological and evolutionary histories, and their species-typical ways of being. Such a position requires openness to learning and gathering information across differences, a commitment to critical reflection, and ideally consultation with people who have experience with and knowledge of the life-worlds of specific others: for example, ethologists, ecologists, primatologists, and long-time caregivers. Being able to answer questions about the specific other with whom one is empathizing can help minimize the dangers of projection as well as the various biases that tend to be associated with empathy.

Another way to avoid these problems is to maintain a clear sense of one's self while nonetheless acknowledging our entanglements with others. Let's turn now to the "entanglement" component of entangled empathy. ❖

Chapter 3

~~~~~~~~~~

ENTANGLEMENTS

*B*EING ABLE TO distinguish one's self—including one's perceptions, experiences, attitudes, and beliefs—from those of another is essential for the kind of empathy I think helps us make our way through ethical encounters. Seeing ourselves as a site of particular perceptions that is different from another's perspective allows us to avoid some of the most serious problems with projection that I talked about in the last chapter. It also compels us to critically reflect on our own experiences, as our own. When we reflect critically on our own experiences we notice how our situation, our previous interactions, and our attitudes, shortfalls, and aspirations are not the same as those of others. This awareness is important for a better understanding of others and an appreciation of a wider, broader picture of the world. In one sense, this all seems obvious. Of course, you and I are different. However, it is surprising how often people think that everyone shares their perspectives and experiences.[41] More often than not, it seems, we are unable to understand different perspectives.

Though very important reasons exist for distinguishing our selves from other selves, I nonetheless worry about the dualism that is generated between self and other. When dualisms become *value dualisms*—distinctions that elevate one side of the dualism and diminish the other, as is the case with familiar dualisms such as nature/culture, gay/straight, black/white, female/male, animal/human—they provide the conceptual bases for exploitative and oppressive practices. This tendency has led some to argue that we ought to rid ourselves of all dualisms, including that of self and other. Some environmental philosophers have even suggested that we ought to create an expansive, ecological self, one that doesn't distinguish between self-awareness and other interests. Deep ecologists suggest that this expansive self generates a sort of ecological consciousness.

I think it is easier for those who have not struggled to develop and maintain a self to be ready to dissolve it. For many whose subjectivity, agency, and experiences have been undermined, questioned, or denied, the maintenance of a self-identity is an achievement and not one that they are willing to give up so readily. The distinction, as I understand it, doesn't mean that the self and the other aren't regularly constructing and reconstructing the boundaries. The distinction between self and other isn't one of distance and it doesn't entail dominance and subordination; it can be maintained in ethical ways. It is centrally important that one has a balanced and clear self-concept to be able to engage empathetically with others. The self/other distinction doesn't reduce the others' value, but rather helps to make vivid both the durability and the fragility of the self in relation to others.

Relational Selves

The concept of the self as an achievement that is distinct from other selves is not the same concept of the self that is operating in traditional ethical theories—the abstract individual who has been the subject of much criticism, from feminists, leftists, communitarians, and others. That abstract self is not only distinct from other selves but is thought to be able to abstract herself from her own situation, cares, and relationships and supposedly figure out who she is and what she wants without reference to any "messy" stuff like cultural, gendered, racialized influences or the realities of embodiment with various combinations of abilities and disabilities. That self is autonomous and independent.

The self I have in mind is not under the illusion that we need to or even are able to escape the relationships we are in. We can critically reflect on the influences that have shaped us. We can evaluate the quality and meaning of these various relationships and explore our dependency as well as our power and privilege in them. This reflection can be a kind of perceptual therapy that helps us develop our ethical skills. The goal, however, is not to transcend the relationships but to understand and improve them, in part by improving our self-conceptions. Our relationships with human and animal others co-constitute who we are and how we configure our identities and agency, even our thoughts and desires. We can't make sense of living without others, and that includes other animals. We are entangled in complex relationships and rather than trying to accomplish the impossible by pretending we can disentangle, we would do better to think about how to be more perceptive and more responsive to the deeply entangled relationships we are in.

That we are *already* in relations should ground the demand for more conscientious ethical reflection and engagement. Since we necessarily exist in relation with other organisms, and since our perceptions, attitudes, and even our identities are entangled with them and our actions make their experiences go better or worse (which in turn affects our own experiences), we should attend to this social/ natural entanglement. We'll be motivated to improve on these relationships, since we don't want to be in "bad" or "abusive" ones. Given that we are already, inevitably, in relationships, it makes sense to work to make them more meaningful and more mutually satisfying.

Inevitability does not entail immutability. Being necessarily in relationship doesn't mean we are completely determined by them or that they are fixed in ways that can't be changed. Recognizing that we are unavoidably in relationships, replete with our vulnerability and dependency, as well as working to understand and improve these relationships don't mean that we accept those relationships as they are. Not all relationships are equally defensible. Relationships of exploitation or complete instrumentalization are precisely the sorts of relationships that should change.

This is the entanglement of entangled empathy. We are not just in relationships as selves with others, but our very selves are constituted by these relations. Philosopher Karen Barad, drawing on her background in quantum physics, describes the self as emerging through what she has labeled "intra-actions." Intra-actions differ from interactions in that interactions occur when there are two or more separate things that come into contact. Intra-actions are what makes those separate things possible in the first place. So the idea of "intra-action queers the familiar sense of causality (where one or more causal agents precede and produce an effect) and more generally unsettles the metaphysics of individualism (the belief that there are individually constituted agents or entities, as well as times and places)."[42] There can be no individuals that exist prior to and separate from the entangled intra-actions that constitute them. But, importantly, the individual that emerges from her entanglements is distinctly constituted by particular intra-actions. Understanding and reflecting on our entanglements are part of what it takes to constitute our selves because there is no self or other prior to our intra-actions.

Entangled Empathy

As I've been discussing, empathy is a process whereby individuals who are empathizing with others initially respond to the other's condition—most likely, but not exclusively, by way of an emotional reaction. There are many ways such reactions can go badly, and I talk about some of those in the next chapter. But they are also often correct, especially in directing needed attention in the appropriate directions. From these reactions, we reflectively imagine ourselves in the position of the other. We can now see that undertaking this requires that we attend to a range of intra-actions.

Many standard accounts of empathy suggest that what

one does when one empathizes is put oneself in another's shoes. But this suggests an account of the self that I am suggesting we discard. And there is another problem— other animals don't wear shoes! What we need to do when we are trying to empathize with very different others is to understand as best we can what the world seems, feels, smells, and looks like from their situated position. To "stand in their shoes" can lead to problematic anthropomorphizing (not all anthropomorphizing is problematic) with animals and can lead to profound mistakes both in judgments and in practices.

That said, we don't want to get lost in their perspective either. Diana Meyers has suggested that to empathize we move between our own and the other's point of view, between the first- and the third-person perspective. This requires gaining as much knowledge of the ways the other lives as is possible. We can then make a judgment about how the conditions that she finds herself in may contribute to her perceptions or state of mind and impact her interests. So, entangled empathy involves a particular blend of affect and cognition. The empathizer is always attentive to both similarities and differences between herself and her situation and that of the fellow creature with whom she is empathizing. This alternation between first- and third-person points of view allows us to preserve the sense that we are in relationship and not merged into the same perspective.

Although everyone is entangled with others and to some extent with various forms and forces of life, not recognizing that there is a particular embodied being who organizes her perceptions and attitudes, a self, can be problematic. We need only reflect on the various ways that those in positions of power have obscured or disavowed the subjectivity of those they seek to dominate and the struggles for recognition that follow to realize the importance of holding onto the self, however porous, vulnerable, or shifting her boundaries may be. Entangled empathy is a way for oneself to perceive and to connect with a specific other in their particular circumstance, and to recognize and assess one's place in reference to the other. This is a central skill for being in ethical relations.

Entangled empathy with other animals involves reflecting on proximity and distance. To do it well we have to try to understand the individual's species-typical behaviors and her individual personality over a period of time. Very often this is not easy to do without expertise and observation. Many, perhaps most, current discussions of what we owe animals fail to attend to the particularity of individual animal lives and the very different sorts of relationships we are in with them. The category "animal" itself obscures important differences and relationships. Chickens, chipmunks, and chimpanzees are animals, but we are in different types of relationships with each. Particular relationships with chimpanzees give us virtually no context for understanding and empathizing with chickens and the same holds true for chipmunks. Theories that generalize over differences will obscure the distinct experiences of others.

Entangled empathy keeps us mindful of differences in context and differences in particular experiences, but it does seem to be limited to sentient beings who have experiences. Entangled empathy provides insight into how we can improve our relationships with other animals, but what, if anything, can it tell us about those parts of the natural world that are so dissimilar that there are no experiences with which to empathize? Those of us who are centrally involved in animal ethics, even feminist animal ethics, may be criticized for excluding vast parts of non-sentient nature—ecosystems, rivers, glaciers, mountains, wetlands. Because entangled empathy involves a cognitive and affective connection to those being empathized with and because it seems odd to think of mountains and rivers as having thoughts and feelings in anything other than a metaphorical sense, empathetic engagement won't happen with these natural entities. Empathy does not appear to be the appropriate ethical response to the non-sentient world.

Protean Entanglements

There is a view that has raised interesting questions about our expansive relationships that is sometimes called "new material feminism." These theories urge us to attend to *all* the material that interact or intra-act with and change us. Though by no means a univocal group, material feminists provide one way of thinking about our relationships beyond sensate animals. Some of these theorists find agency and intra-agency in other animals as well as whole ecosystems and natural spaces, and encourage us to attend to all life forms. Our relations to other organisms are varied and the meaning and significance of particular relations also vary. Some of these relations are more tangible: animals who are in the relation as the eaten; animals made homeless by increased human consumption, habitat destruction, and the effects of climate change; animals slaughtered for fun or profit. Some relations are less tangible—our relations to the bacteria that are a part of our guts and the viruses, and other animals' DNA that are now a part of the human genome.

Being aware of our place in a web of life matters. Recognizing the significance of complex intra-actions among living things helps us focus our sensitivity and provides us with new ways of thinking about our selves and others. When we look at the way that ants or bees live we can gain insight into deep cooperative living. When we study plant life we can think differently about what it means to use others to continue our own lives. When we learn about vast organisms like Pando, the aspen grove that spans a hundred acres, or the Great Basin Bristle Pine tree that is over 5,000 years old, our imagination and sense of time and space are expanded.

Although an appreciation of the complex relations we are in with the more-than-sensate world has important implications, not all relations are ethically equivalent. If we are all parts of bio-assemblages—if we are all companion species, coexisting and coevolving and co-constituting— then an ethic of attentiveness based on this awareness may provide an anchor; but it isn't clear how such awareness might help us navigate through multiple currents. Recognizing life and its various entangled processes doesn't necessarily help us to respond to differences among kinds of fellow creatures. We live in a world of conflicts and need guidance about how to resolve at least some of that conflict, some of the time. Acknowledging our entanglements with the bacteria in our guts and having our perspectives altered when we realize we exist with others that have been on Earth for thousands of years, highlight connections. But these connections aren't clearly or obviously ethical ones. And if they are, the values that flow through them are different from those we focus on when we are empathizing with the wellbeing of an other. Indeed, the focus on these awesome others may actually miss, or divert attention away from, the deep ways in which our emotional, cognitive, and embodied connections are oriented toward those with whom we share or can share experiences.

I can't connect with microbes (even those that are part of me) and although I'm developing a more generous perception of bugs, my connection to them remains thin. I am not moved to act for their sakes if there are other conflicting values in play. I won't harm them and will try to move them to safety insofar as I understand where that might be, but I can't say I am acting from empathy when I do so. I do feel a deep sense of grief when humans fell old trees or pave meadows or dump toxics in wetlands. This grief is largely driven by concern for the creatures that made their lives and their homes in these places, by my one-sided projection of connection, and perhaps by my feeling of "species shame." Clearly, there is value to be attended to in all the places of Earth that sustain life, but they are more abstract. My relationships to the meadow or the wetland or the insects that inhabit them are profoundly different from the relationships I can be in with the animals, fish, and birds who make their homes there. It isn't possible to be in *empathetic* relation to ecosystems or organisms that exist in ways that I can't imagine, beyond metaphor or projection, what it is like to be like.

Intentional Earth Others?

Val Plumwood suggested that a way to be in empathetic relation with the more-than-sentient world begins by understanding the processes of natural systems better. Understanding our entanglement with "earth others," she suggests, is central to our ethical agency. She argued that in order to break down the mind/nature dualism, we ought to recognize, in a nonhierarchical way, that earth others may be thought to have perspectives, too, or more precisely that the complexities of intentionality extend further than we tend to think. Humans and animals are sentient beings to whom we can ascribe consciousness, choice, emotion, imagination, and the like; we are beings for whom life can go better or worse. Given these similarities, we can more readily empathize with other sentient beings. Once we figure out a way to empathize beyond sentience, we may be able to connect more directly with the rest of the natural world.

Plumwood and others focus on the observation that all living things have "life-goals" that can be achieved or thwarted. By attending to a non-anthropocentric and non-anthropomorphic conception of *telos*, we can recognize the interests and needs of natural systems that are very different from animals, including humans. Plumwood writes, for example, that, "Mountains present themselves as the product of a lengthy unfolding of natural process, having a certain sort of history and direction as part of this process, and with a certain kind of potential for change. . . . Forest ecosystems can be seen as wholes whose interrelationship of parts can only be understood in terms of stabilizing and organizing principles, which must again be understood teleologically." She suggests that:

> [W]e can encounter the earth other as a potential intentional subject, as one who can alter us as well as we it, and thus can begin to conceive a potential for a mutual and sustained interchange with nature. . . . [T]he intentional stance opens up between human self and earth others many of the joys, challenges and perplexities of the interplay and exchange between human self and human other which the mechanistic erasure of agency in nature had foreclosed.[43]

We can enhance our capacities to engage with earth others and to understand their "perspectives" by looking to other cultures and traditions, such as the aboriginal cultures that inform Plumwood's writing. These cultures maintained nonmechanistic, nondualistic relations to the natural world. The existence of storied empathy—the ability that we find in children to empathize with fictional beings—suggests that we have the capacity to engage with very different others through narrative, literature, art, and storytelling, and that this capacity, if honed, might help us to engage empathetically with the more-than-human world.

I worry about focusing on *telos* as a way to ground our

understanding and obligations. There are often multiple ends or *teloi* that organisms, including animals, might have, and it is sometimes very hard to identify any one end that serves as an organism's *telos*. But what increasingly concerns me about this path, one I admit in certain moods I find seductive, is that it seems to have us empathizing with the wrong thing, in the wrong ways. I have three worries: first, I don't think it is possible to avoid problematic anthropocentrism with this approach; second is the fetishistic nature of what is supposed to be empathized with; and third, this approach has clear limitations for correcting empathetic failures.

As I have discussed multiple times, we have to take real care to avoid projection when we are empathizing. When we are trying to represent the interests, desires, needs, preferences, etc. of nonlinguistic animal others it is too easy to fall into seeing their attitudes as mirroring our own, or at best, reading their interests, desires, and needs through our idiosyncratic human lens. With beings who have their own perspectives, their own ways of flourishing, their own distinctive wellbeing, we are presented with an opportunity to correct our projections. We might tell stories about trees and rivers and wetlands, but it is always *us* telling the story; we create the narratives. In this way, I don't know that we can be non-anthropomorphic in the project of empathizing with earth others.

The appeal to earth others' life forces or *telos* or biological interests provides some basis for consideration, but I think these qualities are not the things to *empathize* with. They are rational or intellectual abstractions; they aren't the affective or

73

phenomenological grounds upon which empathy is built. We might develop a view in which we come to care about these things and develop duties based upon them, but it won't be based on empathetic attentiveness. In fact, the caring might be somewhat fetishistic. Why should we care about the ends of a river when the river doesn't care about those ends? It isn't clear that earth others have a wellbeing, as such, so in caring about their biological interests or *telos* we are caring about an abstraction, something we might care about genuinely, but not something that they care about.

Taking the perspective of sentient beings, even human ones, is hard, as I've been underscoring. We can go wrong in a lot of ways. Nonetheless, there are ways to correct these errors. Some empathetic failures are a result of our own proclivities and particular personal and political attachment that we can correct. But, as I've suggested, others come from gaining a better understanding of the perspective of the one being empathized with. If there is no perspective with which to compare and correct, then there is no way to refine our empathetic engagement.

The idea that entangled empathy stops at the boundaries of sentience does not mean there aren't other forms of care and attention that could and should be directed at the rest of nature. I am not suggesting that entangled empathy is the only ethical tool. I think many people are in emotionally rich, caring relationships with particular natural spaces. Earth activists have risked incarceration in order to protect the trees and wild spaces that they revere. It is hard not to feel deep grief and even mourn in the midst of a clear-cut forest, and that sorrow isn't simply for those who have lost their homes.

I am in a rich and delightful relationship with the marshes near my house, and not just because they are home to ospreys, bald eagles, herons, egrets, plovers, mute swans, swallows, and all sorts of other animals. I long to hear the rustle of the reeds; it calms me, and the change in the tides has become part of the rhythms of my life. Loving regard for and commitment to other-than-sentient nature is part of a shift in our ethical perception, just as entangled empathy is, but it is not the same as empathy. Entangled empathy involves a process of sharing experiences and perspectives. While being with or even thinking about non-sentient nature may evoke a variety of deep and meaningful experiences in sentient beings, they aren't experiences that are shared with the non-experiencing parts of the world.

Altered States of Perception

Entangled empathy can, and often does, fundamentally alter one's perception. Our perception is altered because in the process of coming to share the perspective of another—figuring out what she cares about, what worries her, and even getting a glimpse of how she sees you—we are changed. This altered perception in turn changes how we perceive going forward, and sometimes that change happens for both the empathizer and the one being empathized with.

My way of perceiving the world changed drastically when I found myself empathetically entangled with Emma, a young chimpanzee. Emma had been raised since infancy by humans with another young chimpanzee named Harper.[44] She is what is called an "enculturated" chimpanzee. She was treated as if she were a human infant and responded much the way human children respond to their parents. Although I believe chimpanzees should not be enculturated and should grow up as chimpanzees and learn chimpanzee social skills, I concede that enculturation doesn't always compromise the flourishing of chimpanzees. When I met Emma, she was still quite young, but had been integrated into a group of adult chimpanzees, all of whom had been raised by humans and those humans remained an integral part of their social group. It was quite clear from the moment we met that she wanted to be closer to me.

One afternoon when Harper and Emma joined us in a wooded area for a walk, Emma ran to me immediately and jumped into my arms. We walked around together, her holding on. She would occasionally get down to play with Harper or look into my pockets or untie my shoes. But she never left my side and either held my hand as we walked or climbed back into my arms. She was so strong and yet so gentle. She sensed that I was nervous when she first jumped into my arms and so she pressed her chest next to mine until our hearts were beating at the same rate. My heart rate needed to slow down, and it did. Our eyes often met in curious and comforting gazes. She made little nonverbal jokes and we laughed.

We interacted a few more times during this visit, and when she was in her enclosure she would often point to me and then to the lock, beckoning me to let her out or perhaps asking me to come in. I shared her frustration when her requests were denied.

My initial time with Emma was so unique and poignant that I can genuinely say I was radically transformed by it. I obviously think differently now about my relationship with Emma, but I also think differently now about my relationships with other chimpanzees, some of whom I know, and some I don't. I also think differently about my own work.

Emma started my thinking about entanglement. I had long been thinking about ways to bridge moral distance and thought that one way would be by seeing how the relationships we had with immediate others who were different could help us expand our perception to even more different others. I have always been deeply connected to the companion animals I live with and drawing on the lessons we can learn about friendship, attraction, and respect in those relationships seemed like a good starting point for shifting our ethical orientation.[45] I still think the skills we learn in our closest relations can help us to make our more attenuated relationships better. But there was something else going on in my early encounters with Emma.

My relationship with Emma wasn't at all familiar; we hadn't known each other well enough to think of it as a friendship yet. I was already in a sort of relationship with her, one that was more abstract and aspirational, which was why I was visiting the cognition center where she lived in the first place. But her attraction to me forced me to realize that someone very, very different from me could form an immediate relationship with me and elicit feelings that I always imagine were reserved for the most intimate relationships. Some of these feelings must have been hers. Upon reflection, I came to think that when her desire to connect with me was realized, that intra-action remade me.

I became much more interested in chimpanzee relationships with other chimpanzees. I started doing archival research to learn about the first chimpanzees in the United States, housed in a colony developed by Robert M. Yerkes. I was able to learn about the incredible friendships some of the chimpanzees had. I developed a genealogical project and was able to identify six generations of relatives in some cases. (I document these relationships on a website called "The First 100," where I also provide information I was able to gather about these initial chimpanzees.)[46] I also wanted to help people understand chimpanzees as individuals and worked intensively to find out who is currently still in a laboratory and who has moved to sanctuary. I am deeply moved to honor these chimpanzees and make them visible by at least sharing their names on a website.[47] Knowing who they are, I think, helps us to understand who we are in relationship to them, rather than simply thinking of them as "captive chimpanzees."

Not surprisingly, I also became a very strong advocate for chimpanzees: not just Emma and the group of chimpanzees she lives with, but for those in laboratories and those in danger in the wild. As I mentioned, I think our relationships with those close to us can help us change our perspective. Many people have told me that their relationship with their cat or dog was what led them to become "animal people." But I already was an "animal person" when I met Emma.

In fact, years before I met her, I was asked to contribute an essay for *The Great Ape Project* (edited by Paola Cavalieri and

Peter Singer, and published in 1994). I declined because I was quite concerned about the amount of attention chimpanzees and other apes received. This disproportionate focus on primates seemed wrong to me when so many animals with tails, feathers, or fins were every bit as deserving of our ethical attention. I was a bit dismissive of what I thought was chimpocentrism when Peter Singer and some of the contributors tried to change my mind. Emma succeeded in persuading me that focusing on chimpanzees needn't come at the expense of other animals, in a way my philosophy colleagues could not.

Once one's perception is altered, other relations move to the foreground. Entangled empathy can occur with those who are more distant. We are in relationships of all kinds with many, many animals and we may never have the opportunity to meet them or look into their eyes. But once we are attuned to some of them, as I became attuned to chimpanzees, we can begin to understand our relationships with and responsibilities to many others differently.

A video online shows a group of chimpanzees who had been living in laboratories in Austria venturing outside into their sanctuary enclosure for the first time. When I watch this video I share the chimpanzees' delight and excitement and nervousness. Some of the chimpanzees had been indoors in the laboratory for over thirty years and watching them take their first steps outside is very moving. I have an embodied response as well as feel relief that some captive lives have been improved. That video has been viewed over 2.7 million times, so I imagine there are others who experience some of the wonder that the chimpanzees experience. For me, watching chimpanzees I don't know experience that first taste of relative freedom brings back the joyful experiences I shared with those chimpanzees I *do* know, when they were moved to sanctuary. And these more distant experiences, with chimpanzees I don't know, energize me to work to help get more chimpanzees to sanctuary.

My entanglement with Emma and the empathy I experience with other chimpanzees that I don't know and who are farther away have also provided me with a very different perspective on other great apes in peril, particularly the orangutans. Over the last two decades, more than 13,500 square miles of forest in Indonesia and Malaysia have been destroyed to make room for palm oil plantations. Over 6,000 orangutans are dying each year as now 80 percent of their habitat has been destroyed. Conservationists are working nonstop to rescue orangutan orphans, and activists are designing campaigns to educate people about the devastating consequences of consuming palm oil on critically endangered orangutans as well as on tigers and forest elephants.[48]

Palm oil is an ingredient in many products, including many processed "vegan" items. When I see a popular "vegan" butter substitute in refrigerators, I have an embodied revulsion. I immediately begin empathizing with the anguish of the orangutans who suffered in order for that product to be made. Entangled empathy reveals my relationship with the orangutans in that instance, and brings together my knowledge of their plight, my feelings of concern, and my responsibility to avoid participating in a system of harm. ❖

Chapter 4

❧❧❧

IMPROVING EMPATHY

ENTANGLED EMPATHY IS a process that involves integrating a range of thoughts and feelings to try to get an accurate take on the situation of another and figure out what, if anything, we are called upon to do. Once we hone our skills, we can empathetically engage with others with whom we don't have direct contact as well as groups of unfamiliar individuals, as we saw in the last chapter. But, you might ask, if empathy is all it's cracked up to be, why is there is so much unheeded pain, suffering, and despair in the world?

Part of the answer, of course, is that many people don't care or are too preoccupied. Our lives are filled with all sorts of distractions and concerns; we are busy and most of us are absorbed in our own problems, projects, and plans. Many of us also have the luxury of not thinking about the problems that most people around the globe and most other animals are confronted with, in one form or another, almost every day. Those of us with relative privilege do not need to worry about being arrested, assaulted, profiled, starved, or killed. We don't have to think that our daughter might step on a land mine while playing outside or that our lover, if found out, will be stoned to death, or that our teenage son will be shot in the back by a police officer in the middle of the street in the middle of the day, or that our beloved campus mascot will be sent to slaughter so he can be served up in the dining hall. Many people just don't want to think too far beyond their living rooms, workplaces, campuses, and neighborhoods.

When people *do* care, that care is often limited to those closest to them or most like them, but not beyond. Empathy is also something we are taught to "get over" or grow out of. We learn to quash our caring reactions for others, and our busy lives and immediate preoccupations provide excuses for not developing empathy. As we've discussed, empathy is also sometimes thought of as a feminine emotion; if emotions are to have any role in our ethical thinking, we are told, we should focus more on anger or resentment and not empathy.

Yet not recognizing that we are in complex relationships that require entangled empathetic responses—responses that include a range of thoughts and emotions—is, as I have been arguing, a mistake.

Another part of the answer as to why there is still so much suffering and pain in the world is that for those of us who care, empathy can go wrong. Understanding the ways that empathy can be mistaken and how it might be corrected will allow us to refine our moral perception. Empathy can be inaccurate in a variety of ways. Sometimes there are things we don't know or perceive adequately enough. These are what I call *epistemic inaccuracies*. There are also mistakes that we make when we try to weigh values in different situations. These are what I call *ethical inaccuracies*.

That some people make the mistake of failing to notice

the desires, dreams, hopes, vulnerabilities, needs, interests, and perspectives of others does not mean that those of us who are trying to empathize always notice those things accurately. In this chapter I will explore the various ways we can make mistakes in our empathetic engagements, and will propose strategies for empathizing better.

Epistemically Inaccurate Empathy

Epistemic empathetic inaccuracies can involve the overestimation of the nature or weight of the others' mental states or underestimating or missing altogether the significance of the others' experiences. In cases in which one is overestimating, the empathizer usually over-identifies with the other. This might occur between individuals who already have strong personal bonds—between friends, lovers, or between parents and their children, or individuals and the animals they care for. In cases of this type, the empathizer most likely exaggerates the mental states of the being with whom she is empathizing.

Consider a mother who walks in the house from work and finds her daughter crying at the dining-room table over a rejection letter from her first choice of college. The mother senses that her daughter is distraught and disappointed, and works out how that feels herself. Naturally, she wants to comfort her daughter, who is clearly upset. However, perhaps because she is overly sensitive to her daughter's distress, the mother comes to feel that her daughter may never recover from this rejection from college and worries about how she can get her daughter through the trauma. But let's suppose in this case the daughter wasn't crying due to rejection at all, but rather because someone she dislikes at school was accepted by this college and she feels jealous. In this case, the mother has misinterpreted the cause of her daughter's distress and also exaggerated its importance to her daughter.

The empathetic inaccuracies that result from overestimating the weight of another's experience are not limited to cases in which the empathizer is particularly close to the being she is empathizing with. Sensitivities to political injustices may also lead people to mischaracterize the weight of certain experiences for those who are traditionally the targets of these injustices. Anti-racist white people, or pro-feminist men, or queer-allies may fail to empathize accurately with men and women of color, women, or LBGT people when they observe or learn about a racist, sexist, or homophobic insult or injury. In these sorts of cases, their empathetic imagination of the others' experiences may be exaggerated based on their identification with the other as a member of a politically oppressed group rather than as an individual who is suffering from a specific insult or injury. This is particularly worrisome in the case of other animals, who cannot easily correct these inaccuracies.

Amplifying the significance of another's experiences often results when one has a heightened sensitivity that blocks one's ability to assess the situation accurately. One remedy for this sort of empathetic failure is greater self-knowledge. When the empathizer becomes aware of her tendency to let her emotional or political dispositions cloud her ability to understand the perspective of another, in principle she will be able to correct this failure either by keeping the tendencies that contribute to overestimating in check (which, admittedly may be difficult to accomplish, but worth trying) or by critically reflecting on the judgments she makes, paying particular attention to the distortions that are likely to emerge. This latter action will be especially important in the context of overly righteous political advocates who often become angry when they feel the harms they witness or experience are being ignored.

More often than not, sadly, those who do not see the insults or injuries as injustice overlook injuries to members of historically marginalized groups. Even those who are attempting to empathize do this. This oversight leads to the opposite kind of empathetic inaccuracy: incomplete empathy. When we empathize with others we are attempting to imagine fully how they experience their situation from their position. We notice the environmental cues that they are responding to, and we try to understand their particular frame of mind. However, their perspectives are often shaped by experiences that we ourselves haven't had, and thus our empathetic engagement will be limited or incomplete.

Lawrence Otis Graham is a wealthy professional black man who with his equally accomplished wife did everything he could to shield their children from racist insults and injuries. He wrote in an essay:

> I was certain that my Princeton and Harvard Law degrees and economic privilege not only would empower me to navigate the mostly white neighborhoods and institutions that my

kids inhabited, but would provide a cocoon to protect them from the bias I had encountered growing up. My wife and I used our knowledge of white upper-class life to envelop our sons and daughter in a social armor that we felt would repel discriminatory attacks. We outfitted them in uniforms that we hoped would help them escape profiling in stores and public areas: pastel-colored, non-hooded sweatshirts; cleanly pressed, belted, non-baggy khaki pants; tightly-laced white tennis sneakers; Top-Sider shoes; conservative blazers; rep ties; closely cropped hair; and no sunglasses. Never any sunglasses.

They developed very strict rules, as many parents of black children do, about how to behave in stores so as not to be falsely accused of shoplifting, where to walk, how to address white people they might encounter while walking, and particularly how to be deferential in dealing with police. One day, as their eldest son was walking near the boarding school he attended in Connecticut, a car pulled up to him and called him the "N" word. In the wake of the violence and brutality that young black men all over the country face, being called the "N" word might not seem so bad. But this man's son was deeply changed by the experience. He now feels scared, vulnerable, and angry. This incident has affected where he goes and who he goes with and has also had a negative impact on his schoolwork and his confidence.

When Graham tried to get the attention of the

administration in his son's school, he received little response. This led him to realize that he was no better able to understand the perspective of the white people to whom he reported the incident than of those who called his son the "N" word. He wrote:

> Try as I may to see things from the perspective of a white person, I can see them only from the experience that I have as a black man and had as a black boy. As we observe each other and think that we have a close understanding of what it means to be black, white, Hispanic, Asian, male, female, rich or poor, we really don't—and very often we find ourselves gazing at each other through the wrong end of the telescope. We see things that we think are there but really aren't. And the relevant subtleties linger just outside our view, eluding us.[49]

And white people in a culture of anti-black racism cannot understand the full weight of years that burden those who experience racism, as well as the feelings of invisibility, rejection, and disrespect that result from it.

If we can't really understand the perspective of other human beings in very different circumstances, it may seem nearly impossible to imagine understanding what a dairy cow or a lab rat or a captive chimpanzee might be thinking and feeling. We are always limited by the resources of our own minds (as Thomas Nagel famously put it)[50]—resources that are developed in response to experiences we have had or knowledge that is available to us. Since the empathizer will regularly lack an understanding of the experiences of others, it seems that empathy will regularly go wrong.

This sort of incomplete empathy, in which relevant details or experiences are inaccessible to the empathizer or when the empathizer is unable to grasp the information that is salient in a given situation, happens frequently. I've noticed it in interactions between able-bodied and disabled individuals. In public spaces that are structured in ways that assume able-bodied mobility, individuals in wheelchairs have an extra burden. When caring people witness someone struggling to navigate the sidewalk when there isn't a curb cut, for example, it is not uncommon to see them move to help minimize that burden by touching the wheelchair and attempting to help. This is a mistake. The person trying to empathize in this case is acting in unwanted ways because they don't adequately understand the situation.

Incomplete empathy can be corrected. The empathizer can seek to comprehend experiences that she hasn't had. If the situation is one that could be understood but isn't immediately for the empathizer, then the empathizer can seek out more details in an effort to correct the failure. It may be that the empathizer is unable fully to embody the perspective of another or completely grasp what it's like to be that being. However, deeper knowledge of the particulars of a situation for different others can help to fill in the gaps that lead to these sorts of empathetic errors. There are a lot of avenues for learning more about differences; for instance, much has been written about the perspectives of humans and other animals from those with intimate experiences and particular knowledge. Spending time thinking and talking about white, male, able-bodied, and other forms of privilege can also be illuminating.

The epistemic empathetic failures I have been discussing can usually be remedied by correcting for the empathizer's gaps in knowledge. Ethical empathetic mistakes are trickier and their remedies a bit more complicated.

Inappropriate Empathy

Let me briefly describe a couple of examples of inappropriate empathy and then explore how these sorts of mistakes may be corrected.

1. *Animal Experimentation and Affected Ignorance* [51]

   Abby does neurological research on cats. She is interested in grounding some of the behaviorist hypotheses in neurophysiology developed in the 1970s. She regularly creates lesions in the brains of the cats, causing tremors, seizures, and other behavioral problems.

   Because anesthetics are likely to have a confounding affect on the brain, when it comes time to study the brains she removes them without anesthetizing the cats. The cats suffer terribly in this research but Abby doesn't empathize with them. They are only cats, after all.

2. *Atrocity, Burnout, and Empathetic Overload*

   Bette has been an animal activist for many years. Like many activists, when she first came to realize the terrible truths about how we treat animals before we eat them, she thought all she needed to do was let others know what was happening and they would change. When she wasn't out campaigning, she was caring for sick and injured animals. After witnessing so much cruelty, suffering, death, and human indifference, her empathy was having a negative impact on her work. She started feeling angry and depressed, and finally became completely withdrawn.

In the first case, Abby fails to empathize with the cats because she fails to see them as the proper objects of empathetic attention. Sadly, our history provides too many instances of failures of this kind—failures that stem from a cultural indifference to certain others whose wellbeing has been negatively affected by failures of moral attention. This error is not an epistemic failure of empathy. Abby clearly knows that cats feel pain and presumably knows enough about them to know what she is doing is contrary to their wellbeing. Abby is making an ethical mistake in failing to empathize.

Some social institutions require that Abby make this mistake for their very existence and thus they have an interest in promoting and naturalizing the failure. Yet, the fact that individuals suffer when whipped, poisoned, tortured, cut into, and starved, for example, is not mysterious or hard to understand, even when dominant social institutions try to convince us otherwise. The failure to see these harms as harms is one of willful or affected ignorance—the phenomenon of "choosing not to know what one can and should know."[52] When Abby fails to empathize with the wellbeing of the cats, she is choosing to accept misinformation about them and thus does not allow her empathy to be engaged by their suffering.

Bette's case is different. Here, because of her proximity to vast amounts of suffering and the frequency with which she is forced to deal with it, as well as the isolation she experiences because of those who cause such suffering, she is experiencing empathetic saturation. Her failure lies in not modulating her empathy and perhaps in not caring enough for herself. Disengaging is an important tool for coping in the face of so much horror. And if she had modulated her empathic engagement she might have been able continue her work and avoid burning out or becoming overwhelmed.

I worry a lot about the effects entangled empathy could have on sanctuary caregivers who have to confront so much death. I have witnessed a lot of deeply dedicated caregivers cut off, even "kill," their emotions in order to continue doing their much-needed work. Urging them to remain open to their grief may be debilitating. Entangled empathy has to have a mechanism for modulation to avoid burnout or breakdown, and distance can be useful in some situations.

Consider Chaz, who has been a triage doctor with the Red Cross for over twenty years, during which he has seen much pain and suffering. As a triage doctor he has to make fast decisions about whom to treat and whom to let die. His empathetic concern for the victims of war and attempted genocide helps guide his decision-making, but he has to disengage so his medical judgment is not clouded and he can continue to make split-second, life-saving decisions. Empathetic distance is central to doing one's good work.

Although Bette, Chaz, and sanctuary workers have good reasons to calibrate their empathetic responses to suffering others, too many people choose to ignore suffering and disengage their empathetic responses to that suffering because it "feels" like overload. Their decisions probably aren't warranted. In a culture in which empathy is discouraged; in which greed and self-promotion (or the promotion of the interests only of those near and dear to one's self) are encouraged; and in which the suffering, humiliation, and the distress of others are increasingly becoming a source of entertainment and even pride, such disengagement should be interrogated. Distance mustn't be an excuse for not taking any responsibility.

How might we correct these different and complicated sorts of failures? Abby's choice represents a failure to take in information that is relevant to her situation. If she is committed to perceiving things accurately, then she will alter her choice so she will no longer ignore relevant information or relegate it to the background of her thinking and acting. Indeed, she will seek out all the relevant information in order to judge how she affects the wellbeing of individuals with whom it is possible to empathetically engage.

The failure in Bette's case does not involve overlooking relevant information or miscalculating the weight of relevant information. Rather, she is allowing empathetic engagement to overwhelm her judgments. She could have remedied that failure by deciding to disengage her empathetic response. In

Chaz's case, his continued empathetic engagement could have negatively affected the wellbeing of his patients, potentially clouding necessary medical decisions. This is a reason for disengaging.

How do the cases of Bette and Chaz differ from those in which an individual has come to believe that empathizing with others is weak, or won't allow him to get ahead in the world, or is childish—beliefs that are particularly prevalent in American society today? The fundamental difference is that, in Bette and Chaz's cases, wellbeing is enhanced by situationally disengaging one's empathetic responses. In certain cases of extreme and unremitting suffering—not unlike those that animal activists, triage doctors, and sanctuary workers experience—continued empathetic engagement must be modulated. Entangled empathy requires attention to the self as well as to the other in relationship, so self-care is particularly important. Not taking care of one's self might impact those with whom one is in relationship. Those who pay too much attention to themselves at the expense of others, and disengage their empathetic capacities because they think it will allow them to get ahead or because they don't want others to think of them as weak or childish, are engaged in a type of empathetic failure.

Correcting empathetic failures and attempting to develop the skills necessary for the right kind of entangled empathy are important not just for the wellbeing of the individual or individuals with whom one is empathetically engaged, but also for the empathizer. Entangled empathy encourages us to pay attention to the things that, absent dulling influences, we ought to pay attention to—namely flourishing and wellbeing. Entangled empathy helps us to deepen the disposition to attend in appropriate and meaningful ways to the effects of our actions within complex networks of power and privilege. We have to focus on how injustice and exploitation work structurally and how those structures differentially impact individuals and their communities. The process of improving our empathetic skills makes us more sensitive and more attuned perceivers; it allows us to understand more completely the relationships we are in and to make them better.

Humility and Hope

Although the precursors to empathy are within us and many other animals as well, entangled empathy is not something we can engage in without critical attention, practice, and correction. I think it is wise to add a good dose of humility to the process of empathizing and the actions that spring from it. In other words, entangled empathy requires work; in that work, however, lie great rewards.

Being in bad relationships or relationships in which we are unaware of our impact takes a toll not just on those who may suffer from our unwitting or mindless actions or inactions, but also on our agency. Recognizing how our entanglements shape us, and working to reformulate our entanglements through more meaningful and mindful choices and actions, are marks of our ethical agency.

The practice of entangled empathy gives me hope. I started this book with a discussion of just how overwhelmed I feel when I think about the egregious cruelties that people inflict on one another, other animals, and the planet. To cope with the feelings of despair engendered by reflecting on the vindictiveness, domination, and violence, I often turn my attention to other animals. I try to focus on the ways they experience themselves in their communities and environments. In these moments of entangled empathy, they buoy me. There is hope in the connections that entangled empathy reveals and reworks, and the possibilities it helps us imagine. ❖

Afterword

ww ww ww

pattrice jones

"WHY GUYS, WHY?" I ask, glancing up into the rapidly dimming sky. Six ducks stand in a semicircle, decidedly *not* going into the barn for the night. As I draw nearer, their reason becomes clear: a young hen, rescued from the roadside only days before, wavers before the barn door, unsure. The big ducks, foie gras–factory refugees several times the size of the small chicken, could—but don't—push past her to the safety of the barn. Instead, they stand between the young hen and the advancing night, allowing her the time and space she needs to orient herself. She does. She steps inside. The ducks bolt through the door.

In deciding what to do that night, those ducks drew upon the very capacity that Lori Gruen would like us to develop and use to resolve our own ethical questions: empathy. Like cows, crows, and other social animals, humans have brains primed to perceive and respond appropriately to the feelings of others—including nonhuman others—but we often fail to do so. Many of us were socialized to devalue or even scorn empathy, as if it were some wishy-washy (and all-too-feminine) proclivity for ostensibly excessive sympathy. Few of us have made an affirmative effort to develop this essential ability, to practice empathy as one might practice drawing or carpentry.

Most of us learned early to suppress our empathy for animals, in order to more comfortably eat them. As we tuned out the bellows of our "beef," we became less able to hear one another. Even those of us who are now animal advocates often remain unable, or unwilling, to "tune in" to either nonhuman or human animals, much less take adequate account of the complex tangles of relationships in which animal exploitation is situated.

Lori Gruen offers a remedy with her theory—*and practice*—of entangled empathy. Providing both essential information and intrinsic motivation, empathy can help us figure out what to do *and* give us the energy to do it. Awareness of entanglement offers even more information and motivation to guide and propel our actions.

Entangled Empathy offers an antidote to the immodesty and anthropomorphism that characterize much of modern-day animal advocacy. Instead of encouraging animal advocates to see ourselves as "the voice of the voiceless," Lori Gruen asks us to actively attend to animal voices, be they verbal or behavioral. If we do this, we may "hear" that the priorities of nonhuman animals differ from our own preoccupations and also that the interests of various nonhuman animals differ from one another. When we listen to animals whom we recognize as being already engaged in the pursuit of their own wellbeing and liberation, we don't get stuck in human-constructed theoretical deadlocks and are therefore more free to be their allies.

That's why I'm so eager for animal advocates to embrace empathy as an essential component of ethical reasoning. I'm also excited by the possibilities opened up by the other piece of the puzzle: entanglement. Ever since I began following Lori Gruen's lead by drawing people's attention to the fact that they are *already in relationships* with animals, and framing interventions as questions about those relationships, I've encountered less resistance from people who previously have been reluctant to think about "animal rights." But recognition of entanglement offers us much more than a useful rhetorical shift. Mapping not only the entanglements in which animals are situated but also our own positions within tangled skeins of human relationships can be a method of coming to understand the workings of that daunting term, *intersectionality*.

The uses of entangled empathy extend well beyond animal advocacy. Gruen discusses one way that inept empathy might lead would-be allies of oppressed people astray. However, the ways that failures of empathy both create social problems and inhibit our ability to solve them are manifold. Social injustice itself represents a profound collective failure of empathy. Lack of empathy also factors among the contributing, if not causal, elements of individual acts of discrimination and bias violence. Without willing executioners who have muted their capacities for empathy, neither wars nor for-profit prisons are possible. Only when humans recover our animal capacity for empathy will peace and justice be possible. In the interim, more widespread willingness to extend empathy might go a long way to mitigate persistent problems in activist movements—such as self-righteous soapboxing and competing in the Oppression Olympics—while fostering coalitions in which felt solidarity in conjunction with respectful recognition of difference spark innovative responses to intersecting problems.

Again, let's not forget entanglement. How might Gruen's insight that we are *already in relationships* with animals inform and enhance struggles for social justice? First, this derails the bad-faith move by which some people use the identities or activities of vegans, or ostensible concerns about some other people's cultural practices or access to vegan food, as an excuse to refuse to reflect on their own participation in animal exploitation. From the perspective of entangled empathy, such pretexts fall away, and the question becomes: What are *you* going to do about the relationships *you* have with nonhuman animals? Are you content for those relationships to be characterized by domination, violence, and disregard? Are you comfortable with the habits of belief and behavior fostered by your own speciesism?

Notice: it's *easier* for people to hear what are essentially challenges to their "privilege" when we approach it in this way. Within activist and academic in-groups, everybody knows what "privilege" means, and we all agree (at least in theory) that one ought to do something about one's privilege. "Own" it. "Check" it. Try to divest oneself of it while simultaneously acknowledging that this is impossible to do. Share it. *Or something.* Although some activists righteously wrestle with the obligations inherent in unearned privilege and do find meaningful ways to discharge them, many seem content to loudly proclaim their privilege before going on exactly as before, seeming to feel quite proud of themselves for doing so. And thus we find ourselves in the age of the humble-brag about privilege. Meanwhile, in the wider world, the insidious invisibility of privilege means that most people, confronted with what feels like an accusation, balk at the very notion that they in any way possess "privilege."

But what if, instead of demanding that people "own" privilege they may then feel powerless to do anything about, we invited people to reflect on their own position within the tangle of relationships among people? Might they be better able to perceive that they are advantaged in some ways while simultaneously disadvantaged in others? Might they feel more moved to try to mitigate any injuries from which they have, however unwittingly, benefited? Might they be better able to see how to do that? I'm excited to see if *Entangled Empathy* can help us to make some headway on the stubborn problem of privilege.

How can you put the insights in this important book to work in your own activism? First, decide that you will. Determine to value and develop your capacity for empathy. Recognize that, like any other kind of perception, empathy is a skill that gets better with practice. Resolve to put some effort into becoming more adept. Enlist other activists in the effort, and reap the bonus of more harmonious organizations.

Here's an easy exercise that serves as a nice icebreaker at meetings. Pair up. As one person shares a recent experience that provoked some emotion (it need not be anything personal—something as simple as missing the bus that morning will do), the other person listens and then "mirrors" by paraphrasing what the first person seemed to feel (rather than what they themselves would have felt in the situation). If they get it right, the speaker feels understood. If they get it wrong, the listener gets the opportunity to see and correct an error in empathy. Swap places.

This and other exercises by which peer counselors, hotline volunteers, and support-group facilitators develop their abilities focus on empathy for other people. But the same skill-set is needed for empathy with nonhuman others: modesty, attentiveness, awareness of one's own biases and characteristic reactions, recognition of both similarities and differences, willingness to revise conclusions upon receipt of additional information, readiness to do background research in order to understand better, and the ability to maintain two concurrent streams of thought (your own perspective and your evolving sense of the perspective of the other).

Of course, it's often impossible to be present with animals with whom we would like to empathize. Thus, empathy with nonhuman animals requires more research and imagination and, therefore, more circumspection before leaping to conclusions. There's another step, too: if you can't listen to particular animals yourself, listen to those who have had the opportunity to do so. What do chimps want? Certainly, you can learn a lot about chimp ethology and then use your imagination. But you ought also find out what Jane Goodall or the folks at Chimp Haven think about that question.

While doing all of this, remember entanglement. Your education or socialization may have, by stressing abstraction or individualism, inhibited your perception of relationships of all kinds. Just as ecologists must school themselves to look for the relationships that constitute ecosystems, you will need to actively look for the relationships in which whatever problem you are seeking to solve is situated.

Fifteen years ago, Miriam Jones and I, in collaboration with a chicken called Viktor Frankl, founded what would become VINE Sanctuary. Recently, Miriam remarked to me that she feels almost as though she has turned into some other kind of animal, with a very different way of perceiving the world, over the course of those years. I feel something similar, although it feels to me more like a homecoming than a metamorphosis. As I hike through the woods to the back pasture, inky-black crows weave through emerald waves of leaves, perhaps on their way to an assembly. Reflecting on what I know about crows while wondering what these crows are doing today, I can't possibly make the mistake of thinking "I'm all alone here." In the pasture, the cow called Poncho can moo very beautifully but doesn't have to do so to tell me he's happy to see me or, conversely, that he'd prefer some privacy. He and his herd-mates can't parse the syntax of my incessant sentences, but do "read" not only my mood but also what I am hoping they'll do. Empathy is, as Lori Gruen says, a "relational process."

Entangled empathy not only allows us to think more clearly and act more ably but also brings us back into a felt awareness of the web of relationships in which we live. That's the beautiful bonus of this way of being in the world. I hope you'll seize it. ❖

pattrice jones *is the author of* Oxen at the Intersection: A Collision (New York: Lantern Books, 2014) *and co-founder of VINE Sanctuary in Springfield, Vermont.*

Notes

1. There are many sources of information about the state of the world. Here are the links to the organizations from which the information in this paragraph came:

   - 2014 World Hunger and Poverty Facts and Statistics. World Hunger Education Service <http://www.worldhunger.org/articles/Learn/world%20hunger%20facts%202002.htm>
   - "Improving the Health of the World's Poorest People," by Dara Carr. Health Bulletin: A Publication of the Population Reference Bureau, Number 1, February 2004 <http://www.prb.org/pdf/ImprovingtheHealthWorld_Eng.pdf>
   - UNICEF <www.unicefusa.org>
   - Global Health Observatory (GHO) of the World Health Organization: Water and Sanitation <http://www.who.int/gho/mdg/environmental_sustainability/en/>; HIV/AIDS <http://www.who.int/gho/hiv/en/>; Media Centre: Malaria <http://www.who.int/mediacentre/factsheets/fs094/en/>
   - "Poverty Facts and Stats," by Anup Shah. Global Issues, January 7, 2013 <http://www.globalissues.org/article/26/poverty-facts-and-stats>
   - "Working for the Few: Political Capture and Economic Inequality." Oxfam Briefing Paper: Summary, January 20, 2014 <http://www.oxfam.org/sites/www.oxfam.org/files/bp-working-for-few-political-capture-economic-inequality-200114-summ-en.pdf>
   - Facts and Figures about Refugees. UNHCR: The UN Refugee Agency <http://www.unhcr.org.uk/about-us/key-facts-and-figures.html>

- Highest to Lowest—Prison Population Total. ICPS: International Centre for Prison Studies <http://www.prisonstudies.org/highest-to-lowest/prison-population-total>

- The State of the Planet's Biodiversity: Key Findings from the Millennium Ecosystem Assessment. WED2010. UNEP: United Nations Environment Programme <http://www.unep.org/wed/2010/english/biodiversity.asp>

2. Humane Society International. Animal Use Statistics, October 21, 2014 <http://www.hsi.org/campaigns/end_animal_testing/facts/statistics.html>.

3. "University of Wisconsin Renews Controversial Maternal Deprivation Research on Monkeys," by Noah Phillips, *The Cap Times*, July 31, 2014 <http://host.madison.com/news/local/health_med_fit/university-of-wisconsin-renews-controversial-maternal-deprivation-research-on-monkeys/article_993e9566-172f-11e4-9063-001a4bcf887a.html>.

4. The Extinction Crisis. Center for Biological Diversity <http://www.biologicaldiversity.org/programs/biodiversity/elements_of_biodiversity/extinction_crisis>.

5. "Doomed for Extinction," by Winston Way, *FMT News*, April 20, 2014 <http://www.freemalaysiatoday.com/category/nation/2014/04/20/doomed-for-extinction/>.

6. Marc Bekoff often uses this expression to move us away from abstraction and focus on the practical. I often use "non-ideal world" in its place because even abstract philosophy happens in the real world.

7. Throughout this discussion I will be using "ethics" and "morals" synonymously.

8. Peter Singer. "Famine, Affluence, and Morality," *Philosophy and Public Affairs* 1 (1972): 229–43.

9. I discuss McMahan's argument and my objections with it in greater depth in my *Ethics and Animals: An Introduction* (Cambridge: Cambridge University Press, 2011). This argument appears in McMahan's "Eating Animals the Nice Way," *Daedalus* (Winter 2008): 66–76.

10. Marti Kheel. "From Heroic to Holistic Ethics: The Ecofeminist Challenge," in *Ecofeminism: Women, Animals, Nature* edited by Greta Gaard (Philadelphia: Temple University Press, 1993): 255.

11. Tom Regan. "The Case for Animal Rights," in *In Defense of Animals* edited by Peter Singer (New York: Blackwell, 1985): 22.

12. Singer makes this argument in many places, but *Animal Liberation* is the classic.

13. Kimberly Hockings, James Anderson, and Tetsuro Matsuzawa. "Road-crossing in Chimpanzees: A Risky Business," *Current Biology* 16 (2006): 668–670.

14. Sarah Brosnan and Frans de Waal. "Variations on Tit-for-tat: Proximate Mechanisms of Cooperation and Reciprocity," *Human Nature* vol. 13 no. 1 (2002): 129–152.

15. Frans De Waal. "Primates—A Natural Heritage of Conflict Resolution," *Science.* vol. 289 no. 5479 (2000): 586–590.

16. Iris Murdoch. "The Idea of Perfection," in *The Sovereignty of the Good* (London: Routledge, 1970): 8.

17. *Ibid.*, 35–37.

18. These are the two categories that are central to ecofeminism, too. Carol J. Adams and I divided our book *Ecofeminism: Feminist Intersections with Other Animals and the Earth* (New York: Bloomsbury, 2014) into two sections: one on "affect"—which includes attention and care—and the other on "context."

19. Lawrence Kohlberg. "The Claim to Moral Adequacy of a Highest Stage of Moral Judgment," *Journal of Philosophy* 70 (1973): 630–646.

20. See, for example, *Animals and Women: Feminist Theoretical Explorations* edited by Carol J. Adams and Josephine Donovan (Durham and London: Duke University Press, 1995); *Beyond Animal Rights: A Feminist Caring Ethic for the Treatment of Animals* (New York: Continuum, 1996); and *The Feminist Care Tradition in Animal Ethics* (New York: Columbia University Press, 2007) both edited by Donovan and Adams.

21. Deane Curtin writes: "It may be that Gruen and I are simply using

different words for the same features of moral experience. I distinguish empathy and compassion partly because I depend on the distinctions found in neuroscience, whereas Gruen adopts terminology from experimental psychology. I also choose compassion because it is clearly understood within the Buddhist tradition, and I see no need to 'reinvent the wheel.' However, entangled empathy and compassion are certainly getting at most of the same points. In most cases we agree." In "Compassion and Being Human" in Adams and Gruen (eds.), *Ecofeminism* (2014): 50.

22. This account comes from Peggy DesAutels, "Gestalt Shifts in Moral Perception," in *Mind and Morals* edited by Larry May, Marilyn Friedman, and Andrew Clark (Cambridge, Mass.: MIT Press, 1996): 130.

23. Jean Decety and Meghan Meyer. "From Emotion Resonance to Empathic Understanding: A Social Developmental Neuroscience Account," *Development and Psychopathology* 20 (2008), 1053–1080.

24. This is a generalization, of course. Some dogs, particularly those who have been abused or had other traumatic early life experiences, do not respond to their people in these ways. Some breeds are not "tuned in" this way. Nonetheless, if the coevolution hypothesis of dogs and humans is correct, their being empathetically responsive to humans would enhance their chances for survival.

25. This view is expressed by Lipps, "Einfühlung, innere Nachahmung und Organempfindungen," *Archiv für die gesamte Psychologie* 1 (1903) as cited by Stephanie D. Preston and Frans de Waal in "Empathy: Its Ultimate and Proximate Bases," *Behavioral and Brain Sciences* 25(1), February 2002: 1–20.

26. Teresa Romero, Marie Ito, Atsuko Saito, and Toshikazu Hasegawa. "Social Modulation of Contagious Yawning in Wolves," PLoS ONE 9(8): e105963. DOI:10.1371/journal.pone.0105963, August 27, 2014.

27. Lamport Commons and Wolfson have suggested that there are

thirteen "stage-like changes" in the development of empathy. While instructive, for our purposes the details of each proposed stage-change are not essential. Michael Lamport Commons and Chester Wolfson. "A Complete Theory of Empathy Must Consider Stage Changes," *Behavioral and Brain Sciences*, 25 (2002): 30–31.

28. Preston and de Waal, "Empathy," *op. cit.*: 19.

29. Of course, there are other explanations for all this behavior that don't require positing empathy of any sort. Kuni may see the bird not as a creature with a wellbeing but as an object or toy that isn't doing what it normally does. She may not be protecting the starling from danger, but keeping her toy to herself. But given that de Waal uses the example as one of cognitive empathy, the anecdote can nonetheless be instructive, even if it doesn't definitely establish that Kuni is being empathetic.

30. These studies were originally reported in Guy Woodruff and David Premack, "Does a Chimpanzee Have a Theory of Mind?" *Behavioral and Brain Sciences* 1(1978): 515–526. I have known Sarah for many years (although not when she was working on these particular theory-of-mind problems) and the observation about helping someone she likes and not helping someone she doesn't like sounds just like Sarah to me.

31. See for example C. Daniel Bateson's research on the empathy-induced altruism hypothesis, which "states that empathetic emotion evokes altruistic motivation to benefit the person for whom empathy is felt." See also Martin Hoffman on internalization and guilt. C. Daniel Bateson's research is published in *The Altruism Question: Toward a Social Psychological Answer* (Hillsdale, N.J.: Lawrence Erlbaum, 1991), and Martin Hoffman's *Empathy and Moral Development* (Cambridge: Cambridge University Press, 2000).

32. Lawrence Blum discusses some of the problems with what I am describing as a conflation, in *Moral Perception and Particularity* (Cambridge: Cambridge University Press, 1994) chapters 9 and 10.

33. Kristen Andrews and I discuss this in more detail in "Empathy in Other Apes" in *Empathy and Morality* edited by Heidi Maibom (New York: Oxford University Press, 2014).

34. Many philosophers who have been thinking about empathy tend to think it does not have a motivational force. I clearly diverge here. Two philosophers that I have learned a lot from, Diana Meyers and Stephen Darwall, both think that sympathy is motivating but empathy is not. Meyers writes: "I propose that empathetic concern is something like taking a humane interest in a person, an interest that stops short of entailing a desire to help but that does not reduce to bare non-maleficence. Whereas empathetic concern for a person jumpstarts and frames the task of imagining her experience from her point of view, sympathetic concern for a person prompts you to respond to her perceived needs by providing assistance." As I've suggested, however, the ability to grasp the subjective experiences of another itself requires motivation, particularly if one wants to do it well. Understanding another's perspective also is necessary to coordinate social interactions. It may be that our social antipathy toward empathy weakens or distorts the motivational component of empathy. See Stephen Darwall, "Empathy, Sympathy, Care," *Philosophical Studies* 89: 261–282, 1998; and Diana Tietjens Meyers, "A Modest Feminist Sentimentalism: Empathy and Moral Understanding" in *Ethical Sentimentalism* edited by Remy Debes and Karsten Stueber (Cambridge: Cambridge University Press, forthcoming).

35. See the discussion in the *Boston Review of Books*, in a forum entitled "Against Empathy" from September 2014 for a sense of their views.

36. Jesse Prinz has a list of eight serious shortcomings, but I discuss two that are most often brought up by empathy skeptics. His discussion of these shortcomings appear in "Is Empathy Necessary for Morality?" in *Empathy: Philosophical and Psychological Perspectives* edited by Peter Goldie and Amy Coplan (New York: Oxford University Press, 2011).

37. In "Fear-arousing and empathy-arousing appeals to help: The pathos of persuasion." *Journal of Applied Social Psychology*, 11 (1981), 366–378, Mary Lou Shelton and Ronald W. Rogers report on a study in which people are asked to watch scenes involving whaling and then showed an attitude change. There has also been a recent neural imaging study in which vegetarians and vegans (as well as meat eaters) are shown images of animals being harmed. The "results converge with theories that consider empathy as accommodating a shared representation of emotions and sensations between individuals, allowing us to understand others. In addition, brain areas similar to those showing different emotional responses between groups in our study (such as the IFG and the mPFC) have also been found to be modulated by religiosity, further supporting a key role of affect and empathy in moral reasoning and social values." Massimo Filippi, Gianna Riccitelli, Andrea Falini, Francesco Di Salle, et al.: "The Brain Functional Networks Associated to Human and Animal Suffering Differ among Omnivores, Vegetarians and Vegans," PLoS ONE 5(5): DOI: 10.1371/journal.pone.0010847, May 26, 2010.

38. Prinz notes in his "Is Empathy Necessary for Morality?" (*op. cit.*) a couple of studies, but acknowledges that this strong ingroup bias doesn't show up in every study. "But, even if only occasional," he writes, "it is something that defenders of empathy should worry about." Simon Baron-Cohen writes, in response to Paul Bloom's use of various laboratory studies to suggest that empathy is actually a problem for ethics: "Bloom says 'empathy is biased; we are more prone to feel empathy for attractive people and for those who look like us or share our ethnic or national background,' but I am not convinced any lab studies correspond to real-world behavior. When the tsunami hit Southeast Asia, for example, charitable donations flooded in from countries from around the world, fuelled by empathy for victims, not based on how attractive they were, and not just for those from the

same ethnic or national groups." From the *Boston Review of Books* Forum, September 2014.

39. Thanks to pattrice jones for the example.

40. Fortunately for the animals, this particular refuge, by paying attention to this tragedy, developed a more skillful empathetic approach that allowed them to begin to see the perspective of the individual animals in their care from the animals' point of view. Reports suggest that they have changed the way they interact with the animals, even though that way of engaging doesn't conform to the ideological commitment of noninterference.

41. In a different but closely related literature, this inability to see that others don't have the same perception as one's self is thought to indicate a lack of "theory of mind" (the studies that Sarah chimpanzee was central in). Children, even after they can talk, haven't yet developed a self-concept and "a theory of mind."

42. Karen Barad's work, most importantly *Meeting the Universe Halfway* (Durham, N.C.: Duke University Press, 2007) has been particularly informative for my view of entangled empathy. I am quoting here from an interview called "Intra-actions" in *Mousse* magazine 34 (2012).

43. Val Plumwood. *Feminism and the Mastery of Nature* (New York: Routledge, 1993): 135, 137–138.

44. See "Chimps: A Whisper Away from Us" for Sally Boysen's work with Emma and Harper at the Ohio State University Chimp Cognition Center.

45. Chris Cuomo and I wrote about the ways that our companion animals can help us shift perspective in "On Puppies and Pussies: Animals, Intimacy, and Moral Distance," in *Daring to Be Good: Essays in Feminist Ethico-Politics* edited by Bat-Ami Bar On and Ann Ferguson (New York: Routledge, 1998).

46. See first100chimps.wesleyan.edu.

47. See last1000chimps.com.

48. Please see The Orangutan Project website pages <http://www.orangutan.org.au/index.htm> and <http://orangutan.org/about/> for more information about the dangers of palm oil.

49. Lawrence Otis Graham. "I Taught My Black Kids that Their Elite Upbringing Would Protect Them from Discrimination. I Was Wrong," *Washington Post*, November 6, 2014.

50. Thomas Nagel, "What Is it Like to Be a Bat?" *Philosophical Review* (1974): 435–450.

51. This is a term Michele M. Moody-Adams uses in her article, "Culture, Responsibility, and Affected Ignorance," *Ethics* 104(2) (1994): 291–309.

52. *Ibid.*: 296.

Acknowledgments

✥ ✥ ✥

IN 1997, I had the good fortune of cowriting a paper with my friend and colleague Chris Cuomo. That paper, "Animals, Intimacy, and Moral Distance," published in Bat-Ami Bar On and Ann Ferguson's book *Daring to Be Good* (Routledge) really kickstarted my development of entangled empathy. About ten years later, Chris invited me to speak at a conference honoring the work of the late Val Plumwood. The paper I wrote, which discussed what I then called "engaged empathy," was published in 2009 as "Attending to Nature" in *Ethics and the Environment* 14(2). I thank Chris for being such an inspiration.

I published a number of other papers that this book draws on and I thank the editors of those books and the presses for the opportunity to publish those chapters. They are "Empathy and Vegetarian Commitments" in *Food for Thought: The Debate over Eating Meat* edited by Steve Sapontzis, published by Prometheus Books in 2004; "Navigating Difference (Again): Animal Ethics and Entangled Empathy" in *Strangers to Nature: Animal Lives and Human Ethics* edited by Gregory R. Smulewicz-Zucker, published by Lexington in 2012; and "Entangled Empathy: An Alternative Approach to Animal Ethics" in *The Politics of Species: Reshaping Our Relationships with Other Animals* edited by Raymond Corbey and Annette Lanjouw, published by Cambridge University Press in 2013.

My paper "Entangled Empathy" emerged from a wonderfully evocative roundtable convened by the ARCUS Foundation. I benefited enormously from conversations at that event. There I first met Eben Kirksey, who later invited me to present my work on entangled empathy to the Committee for Interdisciplinary Science Studies at the CUNY Graduate Center, and I thank Eben, Jesse Prinz, Victoria Pitts-Taylor, and others for their probing questions.

The International Society for Environmental Ethics invited me to keynote one of their conferences in the Rocky Mountains outside of Boulder. An airline snafu forced me to miss the conference, but the invitation allowed me to write a paper exploring whether we could empathize with trees. I thank the organizers for the invitation and am grateful to share here some of the ideas I had hoped to share then.

For the last five summers, I have co-hosted the Animals and Society Institute–Wesleyan Animal Studies summer fellowship. In the summer of 2014, I was able to discuss my work on entangled empathy with the fellows and my cohost, Kari Weil. I particularly want to thank Elan Abrell, Christiane Bailey, Fiona Probyn-Rapsey, and Anat Pick for wonderful discussions about my work.

My dearest Emma and other chimpanzee friends, Sarah, Sheba, Harper, Keely, and Ivy have long inspired me. My human friends who help make chimpanzee perspectives known and who care for chimpanzees are no less inspiring. I am particularly indebted to Amy Fultz, Linda Brent, Jill Pruetz, and the Chimp Haven staff, as well as J. B. Mulcahy and Diana Goodrich at Chimpanzee Sanctuary Northwest.

I have learned a great deal from Remy Debes's work on empathy. Kristen Andrews and I had the pleasure of working together on a paper on "Empathy and Apes," and that ongoing collaboration is the source of good fun and good ideas. Diana Meyers's work on empathy, on selves, and her brilliant engagement with any topic she puts her mind to have provided me with a model that I try to emulate. I feel so lucky to have her as a friend and interlocutor and occasional companion for luxurious meals.

Working with and around Carol J. Adams over decades has been a great honor. I thank her for her support and encouragement for this book and for the wonderful idea that I publish it with Lantern Books. Martin Rowe and Kara Davis have been marvelous to work with. I thank them for their great patience, wisdom, and compassion.

I am delighted that Jo-Anne McArthur granted permissions for the use of her photograph of Rachel Hogan with rescued gorillas at Ape Action Africa, Cameroon for the cover.

pattrice jones and MJ Rubenstein gave me comments on drafts of the book and have also provided sustaining friendship as I completed this project. I am grateful. Big thanks to Dawn, L., Ixaka, and Longo for keeping me company as I was working on parts of this book.

My beloved companion Maggie was dying as I completed this book. Her strength and devotion and her mindful empathetic attention shaped me and thus my ideas. She is a sort of coauthor of this book. Our entanglement continues in these pages and beyond. My debt and gratitude to her cannot be expressed in words. ❖

About the Author

❧❧❧

Lori Gruen has been involved in animal issues as a writer, teacher, and activist for over 25 years. Her relationships with scholars thinking about animals, activists working to protect animals, and with many different animals, uniquely inform her perspective on how we need to rethink our relationships with other animals.

She is currently Professor of Philosophy as well as Feminist, Gender, and Sexuality Studies, and Environmental Studies at Wesleyan University, where she also coordinates Wesleyan Animal Studies. She is a Fellow of the Hastings Center for Bioethics. Professor Gruen has published extensively on topics in animal ethics, ecofeminism, and practical ethics more broadly. She is the author of two books on animal ethics, most recently *Ethics and Animals: An Introduction* (Cambridge, 2011); the editor of five books, including *Ecofeminism: Feminist Intersections with Other Animals and the Earth* with Carol J. Adams (Bloomsbury, 2014) and the *Ethics of Captivity* (Oxford, 2014); and the author of dozens of articles and book chapters.

Her portion of the proceeds of the sale of this book will support animal care at Chimp Haven, the National Chimpanzee Sanctuary System in Shreveport, Louisiana, and VINE Sanctuary, a farmed animal sanctuary in Springfield, Vermont.

About the Publisher

⚜ ⚜ ⚜

L ANTERN BOOKS was founded in 1999 on the principle of living with a greater depth and commitment to the preservation of the natural world. In addition to publishing books on animal advocacy, vegetarianism, religion, and environmentalism, Lantern is dedicated to printing books in the U.S. on recycled paper and saving resources in day-to-day operations. Lantern is honored to be a recipient of the highest standard in environmentally responsible publishing from the Green Press Initiative.

W W W . L A N T E R N B O O K S . C O M